Peter S

Domain

By the same author:

Sheldrake
The Missing Will
A Dubious Codicil
The Stretchford Chronicles
Far Away is Close at Hand
Peter Simple's Century

The Daily Telegraph

Peter Simple's Domain

Michael Wharton

foreword by A N Wilson

NEW EUROPEAN PUBLICATIONS LONDON

Published in the United Kingdom in 2003 by

New European Publications Limited
14-16 Carroun Road
London SW8 1JT, England

British Library Cataloguing in Publication Data

ISBN 1-872410-29-4

Typesetting by KAD

Printed and bound in Great Britain by Antony Rowe, Chippenham, Wiltshire.

Preface

A.N. Wilson

There is no journalist in Michael Wharton's league. This volume is a collection of work produced in his ninth decade. It is funnier, sharper and truer than all the works of his contemporary journalists put together.

In one of the fantasies with which these pages abound, Peter Simple envisages a Pilgrimage of Grace of the 21st century in which a great landowner joins forces with Arthur Scargill. They are cheered on by the spirits of great dead Englishmen — Milton and Blake and Cobbett, Ruskin and Morris and Chesterton. Old Colonel Sibthorp is there, too 'roaring indignantly against the motorway traffic. It is not the physical obliteration of England that they are marching against. It is the monster of Blairite modernisation, with all the loud, low-minded boasts it lives in now and all the decadence and empty misery it will end in'.

There must be many readers who, like me, look to the author of these words not only as to a great comedian, but as to a sage. Somehow or another he manages to be doctrinal without being boring or portentous. I began reading him when in my teens because he made me laugh. He still makes me laugh, more than any other living author, but he also seems to me the most perceptive and unsparing commentator on our age.

Sometimes he speaks in his own voice. Sometimes he directs us to *The Feudal Times and Reactionary Herald*. That newspaper was the only one I have read to make the sensible suggestion that the Ottoman Empire should be restored, together with the Caliphate of Baghdad. He understands more deeply than anyone else writing for the so-called Conservative press that the party which uses that epithet for itself is not conservative at all.

Michael Wharton is truly conservative, and in consequence he finds the world in equal measure horrifying and hilarious. He can say things which most journalists would be too cowardly to write, even though most would think them (see 'A Doubtful Day' p.95). He has a marvellous eye for the absurd, as in his creation of Harry and Janet Nodule, the well-known traffic-jam fans of Turgis Hill in South London; or the letters of Brian Gumbs, reader in Non-smoking Studies at Soup Hales University, with his views on the rightness of Robert Mugabe's attacks on white farmers.

He also has a truly lyrical vision. Witness, again in Turgis Hill, the only remaining oracle in Europe , 'not a stone's throw from the murmuring Wandle'. He takes us through the shrine's history, first mentioned by the monks of Turgis Abbey, surviving the Wars of the Roses, and visited by Johnson, Boswell and Carlyle. 'Today only two elderly priestesses, Dora and Emmeline Pythia-Jones, remain'. 'How to get there: No 284 bus to Turgis Grove. Proceed through Kathy's Pet Shop (decline all free offers); then through the Lord Hattersley Novelty Boutique (ditto), when the broken Doric pillars of the temple can be glimpsed behind the old South-Western Gas Board show-rooms'.

No one else alive could have written that paragraph. It is so funny, so truthful, so sad. This volume will be added to the other, treasured, Peter Simple volumes in our library. What strikes me, having looked back at all of them before reading this one, is that he is writing at the very height of his form, never better.

Nineteen Ninety Nine

A Rap from Kiosk

According to a report in the *Guardian*, the
Metropolitan Police is "launching an audacious
drive" to recruit more black officers by means
of "rap music", a "hard-hitting video" and "post-
ers designed to look like trailers for a block-
buster movie".

Whether or not this is meant as a joke, it has
been warmly welcomed by Dr Heinz Kiosk, the
eminent social psychologist and chief psychiatric adviser to the National Meringue and
Profiterole Authority and innumerable other
quangos.

"It is most heartening," he told a seminar at Leamington Spa this
week, "that policies I have been putting forward for years are being
adopted at last.

"It is essential not merely to enlist as many black officers as possible
— to achieve a true multi-racial balance, 75 or 80 per cent would be
barely adequate — but, far more important, to break down all the false
distinctions between 'police' and 'public' that distort our social conscious-
ness.

'Rap music', particularly if it has a message hostile to the police themselves, should be a basic feature of police training. To make the police
aware that they are no different from other members of our society, they
should be trained in criminal behaviour, as well as being victims of it.

"They should be encouraged to spray graffiti on the walls of their
police stations and help to vandalise their canteens.

"Moreover, as well as recruits from the ethnic minorities, we need
more from all the other minorities: the gay community, the handicapped
community, the mentally disadvantaged, the psychotically disturbed. How
soon, I wonder, can we hope for a sadistic black female 'dwarf' as Metropolitan Police Commissioner?

"That day is long in coming. Until it arrives, we shall have a guilty
police force and a guilty society.

"But" — too late his audience began scraping back their chairs and
rushing madly for doors, windows and even chimneys — "not only do
we live in a guilty society," he bellowed, "WE ARE ALL GUILTY!"

Making Sure

Many thoughtful people are wondering whether Gerry Adams is a werewolf. But how can we be sure?

There are various well-known tests for lycanthropy: excessive hairiness, for example, and unusually developed canine teeth. According to tradition, werewolves can be killed only with a silver bullet (worth trying, perhaps, in Adams's case).

But, at school, my old teratology master always taught us that the one infallible test of a werewolf was that his fingers were all of the same length. Examination of Adams's photographs suggests that he takes care to keep his hands hidden (though there may be other reasons for this).

Mr Phantomsby, major domo to Lord Mountwarlock at his "stately home" in Leicestershire and one of the very few practising werewolves left in the Midlands, comments: "Send Adams down to us at Mountwarlock at the next full moon and we'll soon see who's a werewolf and who isn't."

And he bared his own gleaming incisors in an infectious — indeed, positively contagious — smile.

Benefactor

For the first time, Hitler's personal art collection is on exhibition in Germany. As an indication of his artistic sensibility, it is no surprise.

There are mythological scenes, gigantic eagles, mountain landscapes, stormy seas, armoured knights; also, happy workers on the farm or autobahn, rustic families, good-looking nudes.

At the same time and place, Weimar, another exhibition celebrates the German "avant-garde" art of the early 20th century, the kind of art that Hitler abominated and held up to the execration of the German people in the famous Exhibition of Degenerate Art at Munich in 1937.

However, whereas that exhibition was an opportunity for the Nazis to vilify everything it stood for, the exhibition of Hitler's taste is allowed to speak for itself.

What do the Germans think about it? It is quite likely that the majority of Germans, left to their own choice, prefer the kind of conventional art that Hitler favoured to the kind of art favoured by the present cultural establishment. However lamentable it may be, the same goes for the majority of English people.

Neither the Germans nor the English would dare to admit this. The prestige of "avant-garde" art — which is, of course, mainly, though not entirely, rubbish — is enforced by a kind of moral bullying.

Paradoxically, this owes a lot to Hitler himself. His immense influence on art, as on so many other things, has had an effect precisely opposite to that which he intended. Everything he approved is now automatically condemned; everything he condemned is automatically approved.

As for the innumerable workers in the rubbish art industries of the West — practitioners, promoters, dealers, publicists, critics and all their hangers-on — do they ever feel grateful for their good fortune to that atrocious and unwitting benefactor?

In the Bunker

The troubles of John Prescott, as he struggles to formulate a transport policy, and struggles even more desperately to explain it, is of close concern to two contrasting parties.

One is J. Bonington Jagworth, Britain's most eminent motorist and chief of the Motorists' Liberation Front. For him, Prescott is simply the Blairite enemy of all motorists, an object of ingenious schemes among members of the Front to immobilise him by removing his two Jags and leaving him dependent on a single rusty old chainless bicycle.

But for Harry and Janet Nodule, the eminent traffic-jam fans of Brassgrove Park in South London, Prescott is a hero, believed to be capable of turning the whole country into one great, glorious traffic-jam for the Nodules to delight in. At any mention of his name, Harry begins cheerfully scratching the top of his head where it comes to a marked point.

These two opposing worlds came unexpectedly together the other day, when the Rev John Goodwheel, chaplain-general to the MLF, known to millions as the "Apostle of the Motorways", happened to mention the doings of the traffic-jam community.

"But do such people really exist?" Jagworth bellowed. A strange, most unusual expression, mingling contempt and wonder, and even pity, came over his empurpled face. It was as though he had found a family of Lilliputians living behind the dashboard of his Boggs Super-Yobbo.

Then, recovering himself, he roared: "Smash them! Such perverted creatures aren't fit to live! Can't you put a what's it — an anathema — on them, padre?"

To his surprise, Goodwheel was musing quietly to himself, as, with oil-stained but pious hands, he fingered the gold pectoral spanner that hangs from his fur-trimmed clerical collar.

"And yet, and yet," he murmured. "Do not even these people partake in some measure of automobilistic spiritual truth?

"May there not be, at the heart of a great traffic-jam, at the still point, as it were, of the turning world, a mysterious intimation of the eternal motorway in a very real sense?

"Has it not been said: 'All roads aspire to the condition of the M25'?"

At this fancy talk, Jagworth grew even more furious. But when Royston Cylinder, his crypto-Marxist chief-of-staff, said that to bring religion into traffic problems was to sprinkle holy water over an empty petrol pump, Jagworth, weary of their eternal dispute, sloshed a record octuple "BGA" into his silver hub cap and fell asleep.

Eclipsed

"Perhaps it was that sense of togetherness . . . we all rushed to join in 1997, and that we long for now. We recreate it when we can, in last year's World Cup or this summer's eclipse" (a desperate Guardian writer on the fading cult of Diana, Princess of Wales).

People who hoped to recapture a sense of togetherness by watching the solar eclipse would have been well advised to steer clear of the Stretchford Conurbation.

Its Tourism and Leisure Department, under the dynamic leadership of Sir Elwyn Goth-Jones, had made frantic efforts to attract visitors by promising an unrivalled view of the event, in spite of only 60 per cent of totality.

When rain fell so unceasingly that morning that even the partial darkness of the eclipse was hardly noticeable, the crowds that gathered in lovely, sex-maniac-haunted Sadcake Park were filled with sullen fury. Many of them hooted mockingly at the sky with insulting gestures and demanded their money back.

Mr R. D. Viswaswami, the naked sadhu (Environmental Officer Grade II) who lives in a grotto on the island in the lake, did his best to calm them by projecting some of his most spectacular thought-forms, including one of a dragon eating the sun.

But since it was obviously in the wrong part of the sky and the dragon had a rather foolish expression, they were not convinced, streaming angrily out of the park and pausing only to assault a few sex maniacs who were trying to sell squares of cardboard, with government-recommended pinholes, at half-price.

"The eclipse was a tremendous success," stated Sir Elwyn. "Next year we hope to stage an even better one."

Vote

"East Timor Defies Fear to Vote for Freedom" runs a headline in the *Independent*. That more than 98 per cent of the voters turned up to vote in the referendum on independence from Indonesia certainly suggests that they were defying something.

Fear, no doubt; but also, perhaps a certain scepticism about what can be gained by referendums, elections and the rest of the democratic apparatus.

The intense interest that British liberals take in the affairs of East Timor, one half of a smallish island of Indonesia, has often puzzled me. Why East Timor? Why does it attract such anguished liberal sympathy and indignation — demonstrations, incessant comment by liberal journalists, attacks by Greenham-type peace-ladies on military aircraft due for export from this country for use by the Indonesian rulers? There are plenty of other places in the world that must suffer equal or greater oppression.

I hope the East Timorese "vote for freedom" really does gain them some freedom, whatever that may mean. If past history is anything to go by, it will merely mean the transfer of power from one lot of people to another.

Sensible East Timorese may even think that their best hope of a bit of real freedom would be the return of Portuguese rule, hurriedly abandoned in 1974 after the Marxist coup in Portugal itself.

But unfortunately for them, that is the one thing that they will never get a chance of voting for.

Caring Thoughts

"We want a proper Diana memorial — and we want it now!" "Royal

Family — what have you done with all the money we contributed?"
"Cough up, Charles, or take our undying curses — this is a final warning
— from Mum, Dad, Auntie Pam, Auntie Seanette, Doug, Dwayne, Garry,
Barry, Tosh, Trish, Kim, Garlene, Dagmara, twins Girder and Stuka and
the rest of the caring Gloat family of Stretchford."

These are just a few of the typical messages attached to the railings
of Kensington Palace, with bunches of flowers, by devotees of the late
Princess who demand that her memory be kept alive. Some of these bou-
quets, like that from the caring Gloat family, had what seemed to be
crudely assembled explosive devices taped to them.

Back in Stretchford, feelings were running high. A group of militant
housewives, belonging to the extremist "Death's Head" Our Diana Fan
Club, invaded the Hanging Gardens of Babylon Superconsumerama and
set about dismantling it.

According to their leader, Kay Anchovy, of Kandahar Gardens,
Nerdley, they planned to use it as building material for a worthy memorial to be erected on the spot.

But at a hastily summoned press conference, Det Supt J. S. Harrogate, 52, the police fan club squad supremo, told 700 excited journalists
that the situation was in hand.

"This is mainly high spirits in the run-up to the autumn sales. There is
no racial element," he added from force of habit, his blank grey eyes
fixed on the outsize pork pie on his desk that, for this police mystic and
part-time Zen master, seems to be a focus of spiritual stillness and silence.

Triads Galore

"In my conscience, in my heart, in terms of my personal integrity, I do
not feel stained."

These words of Neil Kinnock, vice-president-elect of the European
Commission and the man in charge of its much talked-of reform, shows
he has lost none of his skill with the Welsh triadic forms.

More, more! He might have continued: "I do not feel stained; I do
not feel sullied; I do not feel soiled." and then gone on for ever.

At the height of his powers, when he was still in British politics, the
Great Windbag often used to achieve a double or even a treble triad, in
fact an ennead, a tottering cardhouse of words that seemed to call for the
applause of generations of fellow windbags through the centuries.

Talking of cardhouses, Mr Kinnock has no more fervent admirer than Jeremy Cardhouse, formerly leader of the Tories for Progress Group, now Labour MEP for Stretchford.

Mr Kinnock's recent statement that the European Commission "has had to come down from an ivory tower from where it produced policy and enforced the law without much understanding of the need to serve", had Cardhouse cheering aloud.

When Kinnock went on to promise "a continual and insistent emphasis on efficiency, transparency and accountability", he had Cardhouse positively squealing with rapture, ecstasy and bliss.

As he swept past on his path of glory, Cardhouse, who was now crawling on all fours and banging his head on the floor, twisted his neck so painfully as he tried to catch the eye of his idol that he had a mild attack of his old trouble, triple convolvulitis, and had to be taken to hospital (sickness allowance, grade one).

Nature Diary

By "*Redshank*"

The first mists of autumn have descended and, on every side, we see signs and portents of the dying year. The mist was so dense this morning that I could hardly see a yard out of my study window, or, for that matter, inside my study. In this mysterious haze, it is easy to confuse one thing with another.

What was the strange, spasmodic creaking that seemed to come from the tall bookcase where I keep my collection of works on country lore? Was it an errant badger, come to borrow some weighty tome, whether to try, with the dogged determination of his kind, to read it, or to shred it for the furbishing of his sett?

Or was it one of those ghostly commercial travellers, doomed — or so the country folk believe — to play solo whist for ever on their folding card-table in the woods, for ever vainly hoping to escape?

Suddenly a loud, booming voice broke in on my reverie. The mist was clearing now, giving way to pale, watery sunlight. Stepping out on the upper lawn, I could see, by peering into the distant fields through my binoculars, what I was already dreading.

The watercolourists were out again in Hoddle's Meadow! Urged on by the big, ginger-headed old fellow who seems to be their leader, they had already set up their easels and were getting busy with their paints and brushes.

By what seems a strange compulsion, these people stream out from the neighbouring town in all weathers to practise their art. All are in awe of the big watercolourist. Some seem in abject fear of him, staring about them with vacant looks, as if lately "released into the community", as the country folk call it; and indeed some of these bony, grey-haired women, dressed in old-fashioned caftans with strings of coloured beads, and those old men with tattered straw hats, bent double with arthritis, may well be.

"Now pay attention!" the big man was bellowing. "One of the greatest of all watercolourists, my old friend J.M.W. Turner, once told me a secret of the trade: first take command of your picture space! Remember that and you won't go far wrong! And here's a tip my old friend Rembrandt gave me . . ." Cowering at his words, they scurried about, dabbing feebly at their pictures till he roared: "Here, let me show you!."

As I walked indoors I could still hear him booming away. Should I have tried to help these poor souls? The country folk believe that even to speak to a watercolourist may bring misfortune. As the old saw has it:

Dunna meddle wi' watercolouring folk
Or 'ee'll be in for an apoplectic stroke.

Fire

The latest victim of the anti-discrimination terror now sweeping over our country and destroying all its institutions is the Fire Service. After the police and the Armed Forces, its turn was sure to come. How long before this moralistic plague attacks the Royal National Lifeboat Institution?

A Home Office review of the Fire Service denounces it as "racist", "sexist" and "homophobic". It is "one of the last bastions of white, male domination in the public sector". All its positive virtues — its masculine comradeship, its regimental spirit, its uniform, its system of rank, its service structure — inherited from its early connection with the Royal Navy — all are condemned.

"It is time the Fire Service began to realise that society is changing and that it is time it began changing too," whines "Mike" O'Brien, described as a Home Office minister. It is his job to say things like this. Most firemen will probably know what to think of it. But what about those who are supposed to be the firemen's leaders?

Instead of speaking up for them, as was their duty, these wretched officials have tamely conformed. "If there is anyone involved in the Fire Service who does not want to turn this report into action," booms an official of the Fire Brigades Union, "they should get out of the way now."

Now it is possible, though unlikely, that after a few hundred years a society might arise in which nobody noticed what race anybody belonged to. It is even possible that after a few thousand years, there might be a society in which nobody noticed what sex anybody belonged to, or whether they were homosexual or foot fetishists or sado-masochists.

If this were to come about gradually and imperceptibly, because most people had come to find it acceptable, there might be a society which, though extremely strange, repulsive and boring, would work quite well, at least for a time.

The society free of discrimination which fashionable doctrinaires, dim-witted prigs and bossy officials are now trying to impose on us, by compulsion and all at once, will not actually come about, nor, if it did, would it work at all.

But while these people are trying to impose it, the police, the Armed Forces, the Fire Service and all the institutions whose proper function it is to help and protect us, will fall into ruin and confusion. The question is: are those who are trying to bring this about merely mischievous, idealistic fools, or are they part of a deliberate conspiracy?

Appointments

Ron Gumbs, Lecturer in Fat Cat Studies at Nerdley University, to be Professor of Road Rage Studies at St Tonk's University College (formerly Cadge Street Polytechnic); Lynn Biles, Lecturer in TV Cookery Studies at Soup Hales University, to be Professor of Body-piercing Studies; Denzil Goth-Jones, Lecturer in Skateboard Studies at Bog Lane University, Stretchford, to be Professor of Advanced Self-Publicity Studies at Lampton-on-Hoke University; Harold Sheep-Harris, Professor of Ancient History at Stretchford University (post abolished), to be Assistant Tutor in Fish Finger Technology Studies at Phosgene Road Sixth Form College, Nerdbridge.

A Nice Coven

Doreen Valiente, a big noise in the modern witch movement Wicca and a pioneer of contemporary paganism, has died, aged 77. She believed in a return to nature and worshipped the gods and goddesses of fertility. Yet according to an obituary, "she could seldom expatiate long on any aspect of witchcraft without giving vent to raucous laughter".

How different from Mrs Elvira Mutcliffe, who runs a much respected coven at Sowerby Bridge in the West Riding. "I'm afraid Doreen and I had to agree to differ," she says. "I have certainly never considered witchcraft a matter for vulgar amusement. It's a question of taste, I suppose. I don't want to be unkind. But I sometimes think Doreen may not have been used to nice things."

Mrs Mutcliffe's own semi-detached house, with its wall-to-wall carpeting, tasteful wallpaper, loose covers and abundance of china figurines and other "nice things", shows how truly refined a witch's home can be. If it were not for the replica Cauldron of Regeneration in a corner of the lounge, the array of magic potions on the coffee table beside the framed photograph of the Great Black Goat of Mytholmroyd, and the presence of her familiar spirit Fluff, a black cat with the rather unnerving habit of quacking like a duck or barking like a dog, you would take it for a typical nice West Riding home.

"Other witches must speak for themselves," she says. "I have never had any time for nude dancing, ritual scourging and that kind of thing. On our regular Thursday afternoon coven meetings, after celebrating the Great Arcana within the magic pentacle in the lounge, we adjourn for tea, with my own home-made scones, lemon cheese tarts and fancy pastries, and discuss matters of thaumaturgic interest.

"Afterwards, we may go into the patio area for a ritual dance. But we always wear mackintoshes or other rainwear so that if it is raining, which it usually is, we can simply carry on. Any suggestion of impropriety is frowned upon. I once had to rebuke Councillor Gogden, who is Keeper of the Trilby Hat of Invisibility, for a suggestive remark about fertility.

"He did not have to be spoken to twice, I can assure you," Mrs Mutcliffe said, as her cat began braying like a donkey and a strange feeling of unreality settled down over the whole neighbourhood.

Extreme

The rise of Jorg Haider and his "extremist" Freedom Party in Austria is causing some concern among Left-liberal thinkers in this country, who fear that something of the kind might happen even here. "The lesson for Britain," argues one commentator, "is simple." It is to steer clear of any system of proportional representation such as operates in Austria.

"We should not forget," he says, "the result of a survey in 1995 show-ing that, in Britain, nine per cent of the electorate would definitely vote for an extreme Le Pen-type party, and another 17 per cent would seri-ously consider doing so."

This is the first time I have heard of this remarkable survey, which, oddly enough, seems to have been little noticed at the time. But we should certainly not forget it now. There is something peculiar going on here.

This democratic thinker takes it for granted that, even though as many as a quarter of the British electorate may hold these "extremist" views, however hesitantly, they must at all costs be prevented from having their views represented in Parliament. They must, in effect, be permanently disfranchised.

I have no idea how accurate the figures were in 1995, or what a simi-lar survey might show today. Is there really such a large body of opinion going unrepresented — in fact, suppressed — in Britain now?

And, amid the sham disputation of Labour and Tory politicians, will it ever make its voice heard?

Nature Diary

By *"Redshank"*

As the early morning mists give way to a golden October day, the mush-room gatherers, mostly women and children, are out in force in the woods and fields, some carrying the traditional wicker baskets that they have woven so patiently on winter evenings, others relying on heavy over-coats with multiple pockets, designed to carry all the fungoid bounty of the season.

Later they will stagger home, laden not only with the gleaming white field mushrooms rightly prized by all, but with all manner of strange toadstools, from the huge yellow bath bun-like Prescott's Head to the livid death cap and red-spotted agaric.

Most country folk have learnt to distinguish between harmless and harmful gifts from Nature's treasure chest. But a few, rashly experiment-ing, find themselves either actually dying or experiencing those "out-of-body" illusions familiar, we are told, to the shamans of Kamchatka. On coming to their senses, these people are apt to feel that there is some-thing missing in their daily lives for ever after.

Old Doctor Mackenzie, who retired to our village many years ago after a life spent among exotic tribes in remote parts of the Empire, is something of an amateur mycologist. But his warning, delivered in many a six-hour lantern lecture at the village hall, on the dangers of indiscriminately eating mushrooms and toadstools has little effect on country folk, who rely on ageless saws and rhymed couplets.

On his own mushroom-hunting expeditions, the doctor has had some curious adventures. He has even had to tussle with creatures of the wild — badger, stoat, viper and even buzzard — for possession of some prized specimen.

Once, near the old ruined, ivy-grown businessmen's afternoon strip-tease club out Hondersley way, he found himself in an "eyeball-to-eye-ball confrontation", as the country folk say, with a pair of dotterel over a giant boletus.

Surprisingly, the will of these normally timid creatures, who, in a tight corner, can rely only on their blank, hypnotic bird-gaze, prevailed and he hurriedly retired.

A great occasion in our neighbourhood is Mushroom Sunday, or "Mycological Sunday", as the country folk call it. On the last Sunday in October, they can be seen trooping from all directions, laden with every kind of mushroom, towards Old Ada Gummer's cottage, for a feast that recalls the grossest excesses of their Dark Age ancestors.

What use are the good doctor's warnings, as young and old gorge themselves for hours, and then, as night falls, sink into profound, hoggish slumber from which some never wake?

Democracy

A British astronomer belonging to the Open University believes that a hitherto undiscovered planet as large as Jupiter may be orbiting the Sun on the outer edge of the Solar System. His theory rests on calculations of the irregular motion of comets in the vicinity.

But other astronomers are doubtful. One believes the object is not orbiting the Sun at all and cannot be a planet. It may even be a mere brown dwarf.

This is enough to bring Dr R.S. Multimer of Stretchford University roaring indignantly out of his observatory and bellowing across the firmament. He was the first of the so-called "angry young astronomers" who emerged in the 1950s to debunk the majesty of the heavens and make rude noises at "all that silence of infinite spaces lark".

A keen enemy of elitism, he is particularly angry at the implied slur on brown dwarfs. He thinks they have always been discriminated against in favour of more showy celestial bodies.

"I'm really pissed off by the pretensions of over-privileged, toffee-nosed planets like Jupiter and Saturn, with their huge unearned incomes and old school tie orbits.

"Brown dwarfs are the real workers of the universe, and it's high time they got their democratic rights in our progressive, egalitarian New Labour cosmos."

Correspondence

Sir — I see that the Germans are ordering us British to end our present policy of allowing soldiers to go on active service under the age of 18.

Coming from the Germans, of all people, this seems to me a bit over the top, when you consider that, only a few years ago they were brutally mobilising children by the million and forcing them into jackboots to trample all over Europe. What is more, I believe they are now planning to do it all over again.

There is only one answer to this typical piece of Germanic arrogance. We should fling the gauntlet back in their fat, sausage-bulging faces and tell them we shall fix the age of soldiers as we please, and send even children under five into battle if it is necessary. As I think it will be, to counter the renewed threat of German world domination.

A. Craggs
"Bashteuton"
Numbe Lane
Stretchford

Provincial News

Nowhere in England is the great beef war waged with greater fervour than in the Stretchford Conurbation. There is a total boycott of all French food and wine. People suspected of possessing either are stopped in the street and rigorously searched for so-called "foreign muck", which is then confiscated and destroyed.

A party of hated "fat cats" found tucking into exotic French dishes at the five-star St Oick's Hotel were rounded up and forced to eat Yorkshire pudding with onion gravy until they begged for mercy.

The council's Department of Civic Guidance has adapted previous warnings about foreign spies — South African, Serbian and Swiss. A leaflet just issued, *French Spies: How To Spot Them*, includes diagrams of the main suspect, a blue-bloused workman with baguette, wine bottle and Gauloise drooping from his lip, in typical defiance of health warnings.

For some of the more educated citizens, ancestral memories are stirring. Boney's on the sea again, and the Corsican Upstart is expected to land at any moment with his garlic-breathing hordes, avid to assault decent British rock stars and fashion designers and ravish chaste British models.

A sign of the times: a notorious "character", Mr J. Hampole, 86, who claims to be a veteran of Dunkirk, has been seen sitting on the pavement, singing that grand old anthem of Britain's eternal defiance of the foreign tyrant, Who do you think you are kidding, Mr Jospin, and beating time with an outsize stick of home-grown celery.

Where will it all end?

Among the Bones

Scientists from the Oxford radiocarbon accelerator unit have confirmed that Neanderthal bones found in Croatia are about 29,000 years old.

This means that the somewhat stunted, stupid Neanderthals may have been contemporary with the taller, more intelligent Cro-Magnons, generally held to be the ancestors of modern humans, and so may have interbred with them. This gives modern humans some Neanderthal ancestry, thus taking us down another peg or two.

But Dr John Goodbone, head of the palaeontology department of Stretchford University, is not satisfied. Bones unearthed on his favourite site near the "Star of Bangladesh" Take-away Curry Institute, on the old Nerdley bypass, are, he believes, no more than 290 years old.

"This means, of course, that most people in present-day England are part-Neanderthal and that most people in Stretchford are largely Neanderthal, as is shown by their stunted physique and low intelligence.

"I am proud of my own Neanderthal descent. It helps me to identify with ordinary people and to play a part in the democratic struggle against the evils of Cro-Magnon elitism."

If

The Government's plan to ban foxhunting, declares John Jackson, chairman of the Countryside Alliance, has "lit the fuse" of a new political movement to defend personal freedom, jobs and services in rural areas. But he doesn't think it will, or should, turn into a new political party.

But with the pressure of events and the Blairite Government's ever-more determined attack on the institutions of this country, the Countryside Alliance may find itself turning into a new political party almost without knowing it. It is no longer just a question of that beguiling but somewhat dubious concept, "the countryside".

A new political movement may be emerging that will defend personal freedom not only in the ever-shrinking rural areas, but also in industrial areas, towns, cities and suburbs in fact, wherever the writ of an alien "political correctness" does not run, and where English people have not yet been forced to their knees, paralysed by neurotic guilt about their history, their institutions, their customs and their race.

The Countryside Alliance, whether or not it knows or wants it, may come to stand for all who see no hope in the established political parties, busily humming the same old Left-liberal tune.

Perhaps the Alliance will take over what still calls itself the Conservative Party, and make it into a party worthy of the name.

At the first sign of such a thing, you may be sure, the "media" would start automatically and unanimously squeaking and gibbering about "neo-Nazis" and all the rest of it.

That would have to be endured with as much stoicism as possible.

World Sport

In the third round of the All-Australia Dwarf-Throwing Championship at the Kookaburra Stadium in Canberra, play between Bluegum Nanobolists and Kissinger Creek was held up for 45 minutes when Creek skipper Neville Dubbo was suspended by umpire Neil Anchovy for an illegal throw in the penalty area (Rule 87), incendiarism (Rule 110), excessive squinting (Rule 124), witchcraft (Rule 139) and consumption of potted meat sandwiches during play (Rule 179B). Result (after extra time): Kissinger Creek 7; Bluegum Nanobolists 5.

Missing

An exhibition of work by Bloomsbury artists at the Tate Gallery has had a somewhat lukewarm, even hostile, reception. There are certainly some serious gaps in it.

Where, for instance, are the celebrated Hogarth Press account books of Leonard Woolf, which, in their meticulous attention to the smallest details of the cost of paperclips and carbon paper, are surely among the supreme masterpieces of the 20th-century book-keeper's art?

Even more serious is the absence of the work of S.J. Barstow (1886-1929), the only hydro-electrical engineering member of the Bloomsbury Group. A contemporary of D.H. Lawrence at Nottingham University, where he was already dreaming of his life's work — a synthesis of art and hydro-electrical engineering — "Basil" Barstow was introduced to the group by Bertrand Russell and soon became a great favourite at Garsington weekends.

Yet there is not a single example in this exhibition of his models of coffer dams, turbine houses and other works, all beautifully executed in matchwood, which Virginia Woolf found so "subtly, evanescently amusing", which made Lytton Strachey swoon with emotion and Ottoline Morrell fall deeply, though transitorily, in love with the awkward young engineer.

A favourite's reign is often brief. Barstow's demonstrations of his art went too far. When he passed a high-voltage current through Virginia's handbag, setting it on fire, the Bloomsberries turned against him. Duncan Grant cut him dead. Strachey tittered and pointed at him most woundingly.

Soon even his only remaining friend, the formidable composeress Ethel Smyth, whose booming, surging voice reminded him of "the sudden release of a million gallons of water from some stupendous mountain reservoir", deserted him. He took the only way out, ending his brief life by auto-hydro-electrocution.

Social Problem

The Chancellor's promise to give pensioners aged over 75 free television licences next autumn has flung the Stretchford Conurbation into turmoil.

It is estimated that there are more really dedicated television-watchers there — people who watch the screen literally all the time, even when their sets are out of order — than in any other major centre of population. Social psychologists believe that free licences for pensioners over 75 will have a "profound effect on demographic and behavioural patterns". Families that at present regard their older members as at best "boring" and at worst "an intolerable nuisance" will now begin to regard them as an asset. According to a survey, 23 per cent of families are prepared, if necessary, to invent an imaginary old person (the "phantom pensioner syndrome") in order to claim a free licence.

Seventeen per cent would be prepared to kidnap pensioners and install them in their homes. A potential threat to law and order is the emergence of professional kidnapping gangs, who will snatch up old people in the streets at random and sell them to families who, in their unbridled lust for free television, will pay a very high price for them.

Three per cent say they will "chain the old beggars down" or shut them up in cupboards to prevent them from escaping. How do the civic authorities view this new threat to human rights? Will a new form of slavery emerge in the 21st century?

Empire

A new code of conduct to replace the present ban on homosexuals in the Services, designed to placate the law-givers of "Europe", approaches the borders of dementia.

It forbids touching, displays of affection or love affairs across the ranks, even between people of opposite sex. Anticipating objections from the Services themselves, Geoffrey Hoon, described as a Defence Secretary, says he wants "a revised policy that sustains operational effectiveness".

For liberal thinkers, operational effectiveness, except perhaps for "ethical" or "peacekeeping" operations, has a low priority. The main requirement is that the Services should fit in with a society in which all forms of "sexual orientation" are equally acceptable. To bring this about, the same methods of pseudo-moralistic bullying will be used as are used in trying to expunge "racism" in the Services.

In the case of "sexuality", the difficulties may be even greater. A special Army Directorate of Sexual Orientation will have to be set up. This will offer a glorious opportunity for the classic service exercise of "empire building" on a scale hitherto unknown. How many thousands of sexual orientation staff officers and other ranks will be needed?

How many psychological officers, sexological officers, sex educational officers? How many officers for the legal branch of the directorate to deal with innumerable complex disciplinary cases and claims for compensation? As the new directorate expands its operations ever wider, it will make any other operations virtually impossible.

Liberal opinion will at last have the sort of Army it has always wanted. Provided all other countries follow suit, world peace will be ensured for ever.

Past and Present

The first of a new kind of municipal official, whose job will be to "boost civic leadership", has been appointed. A dynamic young advertising executive, he "will apply business techniques to regeneration", deal with the "media" and promote tourism.

Perverse fate has decreed that the first city to acquire what is described as a "city spin doctor" who will "sell it as a product" should be Bradford.

Most people will wonder what Alderman Foodbotham, the crag-jawed, iron-watch-chained, grim-booted perpetual chairman of the Bradford City Tramways and Fine Arts Committee in the great days would think of this latest innovation among so many. Would he, in his own accustomed phrase, "take no cognisance" of it whatever?

For him, Bradford, with its resounding trams, its soot-black town hall whose bell-booming towers pierced the rainy skies, its stupendous warehouses and enchanted Wool Exchange, was a personal trust, a city that was its own justification, requiring no other. He would have seen no reason to sell or promote or regenerate it.

He had never heard of "tourism" and would have been surprised if anyone had wanted to visit Bradford except on business. He would have thought a "spin doctor" must be one of those itinerant touts offering fraudulent cures for indigestion or dizzy spells, at the annual municipal clerks' hiring fair.

As he lies, according to legend, in his mountain cave at Northowram, awaiting the summons by magic horn, mill hooter or other instrument to wake, to board his ceremonial tram and ride forth to save the city at the last hour, when business techniques and media and products alike will be swept away like noxious vapours, what can such base, newfangled phenomena be for him but shifting phantoms in his troubled dreams?

Spin

The techniques of "spin doctoring" have been practised since ancient times. What seems to be new is that the practice has become generally known to the public, its victims, and even accepted by them.

So when the Blairs announce they are going to have a baby, many people assume that the announcement has been carefully timed to divert attention from something else, the threat of Ken Livingstone, for example, or a momentary rise in the standing of William Hague. It is assumed that the fall of Jeffrey Archer has been timed to give the Blairites further advantage.

It is even assumed that the Queen's award of the George Cross to the Royal Ulster Constabulary has been timed, probably by the arch-spin doctor Peter Mandelson, to help David Trimble get Unionist approval for the proposed deal in Northern Ireland.

Because this last assumption of "spin" involves, instead of a lot of politicians engaged in their customary manoeuvres, a body of brave men doing their duty in the face of real danger and death, it belongs to an altogether different order of shame and repugnance.

But it is equally part of the degradation of public life in an engulfing cynicism. When nobody can any longer believe anything he is told, except that anything he is told is likely to be a part of a self-seeking conspiracy, will he stop believing anything at all?

And what will be the eventual outcome of that? A mindless indifference? Or an outbreak of ungovernable rage?

A Bishop's Life

A report, called *To Be A Bishop*, issued just before the Church of England Synod, outlines the working life of bishops and explains how their stipends and expenses are accounted for.

There had been threats from certain "traditionalist clergy" to publish details of the expenditure of different bishops on palaces, chauffeurs and so on, and of the disparities between them.

"This is yet another proof," says Dr Spacely-Trellis, the go-ahead Bishop of Stretchford and Bevindon, "of the utter irrelevance of those miserable, lingering traditionalist elements in a Church that, in spite of everything, is trying to come to terms with the financial ideals of the average man and woman seeking a meaningful religion in our secular society."

Dr Trellis does not attend the Synod himself, because of its partial recognition of the supernatural. But he agrees with its more forward-looking views and is particularly enraged by any attempts to publicise details of his own diocesan expenditure. He gave up the rambling mediaeval bishop's palace years ago (it is now a "family planning" clinic) and lives with his partner, the  Rev Mantissa Shout, a militant feminist, at the "Bishop's Squat" in Ecumenical Road, Stretchford.

It is twice as large as the old palace, with offices, library and computer centre, conference hall with five-star accommodation, restaurant and nine-hole golf course, rock music centre, gymnasium, sex cinema, mosque, Hindu temple and "all-faith facilities".

With his multifarious public commitments and advisory posts — such as his chairmanship of Football Managers for a Multi-faith Millennium — his own rock group, Chocolate Meringue Narthex, and his virtually non-stop appearances with his partner on television, his life is by no means austere.

"Though modest," he says, "our lifestyle is adequate for a modern bishop in a very real sense."

A Moving Story

I was sorry to hear of Jeffrey Archer's troubles. I don't think I ever met him, but by all accounts he seems to be an amiable, amusing and generous fellow.

I have read somewhere that he is a "victim of Tory snobbery". Considering the sort of people now in the Tory party who were once his friends but have now dropped him, this does not seem likely.

I am told he has often been guilty of fibbing about his own achievements. But I can hardly believe he ever went so far, as I have been told he did, as to claim to have been a guest at Simpleham several times in the past 20 years.

But if he really did make this absurd claim, it is quite creditable to him in a way. It is always wrong to fib, of course. But a fib of this magnitude indicates such lofty, unfulfillable aspirations in the fibber that it would seem moving and forgivable.

Well Done!

Among the millions of nauseating words that have been printed about the Blairs' baby, the following extract from a reader's letter in the *Independent* deserves a handsome prize for combining priggishness, offensiveness, stupidity and a mind-numbing addiction to progressive clichés and popular fallacies:

"We can deplore the selfishness of our nation's leading couple in having a fourth child at a time when the world's population is continuing to grow at an unsustainable rate, and their irresponsibility in enjoying recreational sex without adequate contraception, when just that behaviour results in our having the highest rate of teenage pregnancies in Europe."

Babylon

Beware of the dreams of your youth; they may be fulfilled in old age. Are those doctrines of Luddite Fundamentalism, expounded in many a wistful paragraph in this column through the ages, now unwelcomely enacted in a carnival of violence on the streets of London and Seattle?

Think of all those grotesque demonstrators in America — those anarchists, ecolepts, protectors of trees and animals and partisans of reactionary Tibet — with their masks and effigies of "endangered species", dolphins and whales and turtles, their weird, exotic banners. Was the old green banner of Captain Ludd raised among them?

Think of those somewhat less fantastic demonstrators in London where, none the less, a police van they overturned and set on fire bore the resounding slogan "Babylon Falling Down". Imagery from the Scriptures mingles with the modish jargon of environmentalists and cloudy-headed animal rights fans: Babylon, "that great city, mother of harlots and abominations of the earth", has become the symbol of global capitalism, the new world order of Mammon that Clinton and Blair pronounce inevitable and irresistible.

That simple columnar dream was of peasants tearing down the satanic factories and laboratories with their bare hands, to restore a wild, green England like that of Richard Jefferies's *After London*, with its feudal rulers and earthbound people. But the overthrow of our modern Mammon-Babylon, with its ever more elaborate technology, its magic web of lies spun round the world, would be terrible beyond imagination.

High Hopes

As Minister of Education in Northern Ireland, Martin McGuinness (or Máirtin Mac Aonghusa, as he must now, in all decency, spell his name) will have a good opportunity of promoting the Irish language. He may perhaps think it premature to make it compulsory in schools straight away; but that must surely be the eventual object.

With the greater toughness, determination and efficiency of the Ulster people, it should be possible to carry out the policy of restoring the language which has failed so lamentably in the Republic, and so, by setting an example, shame the people of the South into following suit.

Once they have got over their prejudice against a language which is equally theirs as Irishmen, the Unionists will no doubt co-operate. There must be many of their not-so-remote ancestors who, in the continual movement of peoples from Ireland to Scotland and back again, were Gaelic speakers in their day.

As the language of all-Ireland, the Gaelic will take its proper place in the councils of Europe, adding its noble and melodious voice to deliberations in Brussels and Strasbourg from which it has hitherto been so shamefully excluded, and releasing, through hordes of eager translators, glorious new cyclones of superfluous paper.

The time may come when words of command in the tongue Cuchulain spoke ring out with martial clangour on the parade grounds of Blair's New Model Labour European Army, as it prepares for peacekeeping operations more terrifying and atrocious than any so far known.

Lost

Almost without my being aware of it, a grim, croaking sound came from my thin lips, while a rictus that might just have been taken for a smile passed over my impassive features.

I was reading about the failure of the latest attempt to land a spacecraft on Mars, and looking with equal pleasure at pictures of American scientists hanging about listlessly in their gadget-crammed headquarters, with forlorn expressions on their rather stupid but normally cheerful faces.

For the time being, the hope, trumpeted in many a frenzied newspaper article, that Man was about to begin a new stage of his development by colonising first Mars, then the whole solar system, then the whole universe, has come to nothing.

The idea of exporting our hideous technological culture to other worlds and inflicting on them the fate that has already ravaged our own earth from end to end has been postponed.

The space maniacs of Nasa and their innumerable admirers will try again. They may yet see their evil-looking machines grubbing up the planets for their mineral wealth and transmitting to their gleeful ears all the information they need for carrying on the process indefinitely.

What have these mad dreams of conquering the universe to do with the real concerns of living, breathing, feeling, suffering human beings?

Round the Clubs

How will the Blairites' proposed ban on all-male clubs (writes "Clubman") affect the Old Thanateum ("Thanners") in Pall Mall? It is already in difficulties through taking in too many members of other clubs that have lost their own premises, such as the Geologists ("Jollers"), the Philologists ("Floggers") and Peppers ("Peppers").

"The fact is," Major "Jock" Gapwright-Jones ("Gappers"), the club secretary, tells me, "we have no rule against women members. We just don't seem to have any. Yet we've fallen over backwards to accommodate them. For instance, they may use the library at any time when there is nobody else in it."

A glance through the open door showed that the library was crowded with members, some of them even sitting high up in the bookshelves and clinging precariously to the ceiling. Some looked as though they had been there for centuries and were beginning to curl at the edges.

"What more can these women want?" asked "Gappers". He broke off in a fit of coughing, in which I joined, as Jim, the club's much-loved pet wyvern, came trotting up the great staircase, setting fire to it with his fiery breath. "Do you think fabulous monsters put them off?

"Actually, our main problem is not lady members, but this chap from Westminster Council who keeps coming round and warning me that Jim is a fire hazard. Yesterday another council chap came round to say that Jim was a food safety hazard as well. Of course, Jim has the run of the kitchens and sometimes lends a hand, as it were, with our famous savouries, devilled bones and what have you.

"And would you believe it, while we were talking, another council chap, this one with two sidekicks, appeared and said the club was a bad case of overcrowding and an environmental health hazard. As it happened,

Jim sauntered up just then and set fire to this chap's briefcase.

"You couldn't see their feet for dust," "Gappers" chuckled, as a paroxysm of coughing seized us both. Through the smoke I noticed that Bousfield ("Boffers"), the head steward, had burst into flames in his dignified, respectful way.

Christmas Reading

Outstanding among children's fiction this Christmas is *Jill of Numbe Lane* by Dee Ogreburg (Viper and Bugloss, £12.99). Dee is the adopted daughter of the great Marylou Ogreburg, founder of the Bread and Marmite Multiracial People's Street Dance Theatre.

Jill Boldheart, an eight-year-old opponent of Section 28, is a star pupil at Numbe Lane Primary School. Thanks to her pioneering work, the 30-odd boys and girls in her class have dropped conventional lessons altogether and spend their whole time in discussion groups, coming to terms with their sexuality.

Fortunately, Jill and her friends manage to frustrate the efforts of an evil teacher, Howard Scumbag, a Tory reactionary with a ginger moustache, to teach them irrelevant subjects like reading. Eventually, they all come to terms with their sexuality, mostly turning out bisexual, with a few exclusive homosexuals.

When Mr Scumbag threatens to "exclude" Jill, she exposes him as a "homophobic bully" and secret foxhunter. The story reaches a thrilling climax when she solves a mystery: how did the portrait of Tony Blair, the Dear Leader, come to be removed overnight from its place of honour on the classroom wall?

It turns out that the culprit is Mr Scumbag himself! Disgraced, he is himself "excluded" by Jill. He has a well-deserved nervous breakdown, and ends up taking refuge with fellow fascists at a sinister ruined golf club.

Down the Mineshaft

"Here's a Christmas present for thi, lad!" Julian Birdbath, Last Citizen of the Republic of Letters and discoverer of the so-called "Missing Bronte Sister", Doreen, winced painfully as the voice of Mr Shuttleworth, the West Riding-born poultry farmer and part-time literary agent, came booming down the shaft to Number Two Level, Deadwater Leadmine (disused), near Bakewell, where he sat huddled over his rusting typewriter, working on his life of Stephen Spender.

A bulky, sodden object wrapped in brown paper, with a much-reused Christmas label on it, came hurtling down the shaft. Opening it with numbed fingers, Birdbath found a copy of a newly published book by a David Lemming. It was a biography of Stephen Spender himself!

"Happen it'll help thi in thi work — and happen not! Happen it'll make it into a right work of supererogation!" Mr Shuttleworth bellowed, pronouncing the word slowly and with relish.

And, with a triumphant rattle of his hen-feed bucket, this kindly man tramped back over the snowy upland to the company of his hens by his own warm, comfortable fireside.

Birdbath scarcely had the heart to open the book. Would it really make all those years of work superfluous? But what did that matter in the end? The readiness is all.

With a supreme effort of will, he bent once more over the familiar sodden, disintegrating papers. The tall, gangling figure of Spender himself seemed to rise and brood over him, shimmering amid the gloom in an irritating way.

As the doomed author glanced round the dripping walls, a gust from the surface whistled through the rusting machinery and a large stalactite suddenly crashed to the floor, just missing his head.

He gave a deep groan, as Amiel, his pet toad and sole companion, scrambled on to his typewriter and peered trustingly into his face.

Moved by the devotion of this humble creature, he pressed on with his unending task. Where was he? Yes, Spender's third circumnavigation of the globe, when he broke his own record by attending more literary conferences than all the other writers in history put together . . . New Guinea Book Festival of 1974: Whither the Novel? . . .

Christmas Reading

Among the annuals, this year's *Bumper Book of Anti-Racism* (Ethnicaids Press, £20) is even better than ever! Edited by Tamsin Alibi-Jones, the dynamic director of the Race Relations Industrial Council, it is a real feast of good things for young and old!

Here are hints by eminent experts on how to detect racism in thousands of everyday things, from bus timetables, lawn mowers, soap dishes, tennis rackets, corkscrews and bath buns to teddy bears and plastic ducks. Here are hints for the elderly on how to build a DIY race relations outreach workshop from easily available materials without stirring from their armchairs. There are fascinating new games on anti-racist themes, such as anti-racist ludo, providing hours of fun for all the family.

In a more serious vein, there are dozens of articles on such fascinating subjects as the Aztecs of Nerdley. Royston Huitzilopochtli (formerly Royston Nobes), a South Shields-born 40-year-old sociology student at Nerdley University, tells how he constructed, almost single-handed, an Aztec ethnic community whose very existence has been disputed by malicious racists, but which has become a powerful inspiration for our multiracial society.

Two Thousand

Problem Corner

Dear Clare Howitzer — I am in my early thirties, slightly bald, with a degree in non-smoking studies at Soup Hales University, at 15 stone rather overweight for my height (5ft) and am generally considered quite attractive. I work in a dead-end job as a software cataloguer at a toothbrush hire agency and, as I am a  committed socialist and a keen admirer of Tony Blair, I would like to be a Labour MP and one of "Blair's Babes".

I wrote to my constituency association with 11 copies of my CV, but received only a formal acknowledgement. When I called there in person, wearing my smart rust-coloured "power dressing" outfit, with the new, matching "in-yer-face" make-up, set off by long silver "ball-and-chain" earrings, the receptionist fainted and I was shown out by a brutal, male chauvinist porter. I wrote to complain to Tony himself, but got no reply.

How can I make the party realise that I have a vital contribution to make as a New Labour MP?

(Sandra Gropes, Nerdley).

Clare Howitzer replies: There are a lot of idealistic young women like you, Sandra, anxious to help with the task of changing this stuffy old Tory-fixated Britain and making it a better, fairer country.

Have you thought of taking a course in New Labour feminist self-assertiveness? If you still cannot get the party to appreciate you as you deserve, I can recommend an agency that teaches kung fu, Malaysian kick-boxing and, on its advanced course, the techniques of armed ambush and applied terrorism. Good luck, dear.

A Great Debate

In a stormy debate, Nerdley Borough Council discussed a motion by Cllr Don Binliner (Lab) to approach Grozny Town Council with a view to twinning.

"I have always had a soft spot for Grozny," he said, "ever since I visited it with my wife and a party of committed socialists in the halcyon days of the old Soviet Union.

"We had a wonderful time, staying at the Grand Central Lenin Hotel, inspecting the magnificent housing estates, schools and hospitals, and exchanging views on world peace with local officials.

"We got on particularly well with the so-called secret police, whose methods of dealing with enemies of the people, so different from anything we had in Nerdley, struck us as most interesting.

"As far as we are concerned, the bond between our two towns is still strong. There is some trouble in Grozny at present, no doubt due to misunderstandings got up by enemies of the people.

"Basically, they are the same enemies we face in Nerdley, Tory reactionaries dedicated to bringing back the bad old days of feudal oppression.

"But just as the people of Grozny have fought back, so have we Nerdley people. We can point to our proud achievements in declaring Nerdley a nuclear-free zone, and, later on, a foxhunting-free zone.

"Now my wife and I are looking forward to resuming our cordial dialogue with the Chechen people."

Cllr Frank Holehead (Con): "I am all in favour of Cllr and Mrs Binliner going to Grozny as soon as possible and staying there. I hope they have an interesting and exciting time. But I hope we don't get any Chechens coming here. Cllr Binliner's Kosovo Albanian friends of last year were bad enough. Chechens might be even worse."

Cllr Binliner: "That is the most despicably racist remark I have ever heard, even from a drunken buffoon like Cllr Holehead. He should be ashamed of himself. I only wish some Chechens were here now to deal with him as only they would know how."

(Uproar in which the speaker joined.)

Distressing

For reasons only too lamentably obvious, that admirable charity the Distressed Gentlefolks' Aid Association has changed its name to something more acceptable in our dismal times.

Since time immemorial, it has used an advertisement showing an old gentleman in his lonely room, looking mildly distressed but absorbed in chess problems, with the caption: "I thought I'd have enough, but these days one has to have help."

Will this moving scene also have to go? What will the old gentleman be doing in a new, up-to-date advertisement? Watching television?

For his soul's sake, it would be better to show him doing literally anything rather than that: playing noughts-and-crosses against himself, for instance, or cutting the buttons off his coat and sewing them on again.

Why, Oh Why?

Anger, intangible yet unmistakable (writes a special correspondent) is growing daily in the Stretchford Conurbation, threatening an explosion of indignation that could well turn into a cataclysm of uncontrollable wrath.

Why, people are asking more and more insistently, are there no rumours of lynch mobs roaming the city in search of black victims? Why are other places always in the news? What have they got that Stretchford hasn't?

Why are there no crowds of reporters seeking interviews with the families of black victims? Why are there no exciting news conferences? Why have no "human rights" lawyers descended on the city? Why has Paddy Ashdown not spoken against racism in Stretchford? Why have the police not been satisfactorily pilloried for neglecting to carry out their investigations properly? Why have they not promised a public inquiry into their behaviour?

Council officials point out that none of these things has happened because no black people have perished in suspicious circumstances, or even in circumstances that anybody could possibly think suspicious. But ordinary people, particularly "human rights" activists and professional anti-racists, are not taking this for an answer.

At a crowded public meeting in the Sadcake Memorial Hall, scene of so many stirring protests through the ages, Mrs Norma Globes, a prominent activist, called for immediate action.

"Stretchford cannot afford to fall behind in this vital field of human endeavour," she said. "When I think of what other cities — even small towns and villages — have achieved, I feel ashamed. Everywhere you look in Stretchford you can see policemen with big fat smiles on their faces, looking as innocent as you please. It is up to us to change all that and have them not just apologising, but grovelling," she added to tumultuous applause.

Her Committee for Racial Justice has approached Ken Slabb, the perpetual president of the students' representative council at Stretchford University and commander-in-chief of the demonstrational forces, for help in organising a protest march on the Civic Centre.

But Slabb, though nominally in command of four divisions of militant students, with support groups including Pixie Dutt-Pauker's crack feminist shock troops, can no longer rely on their discipline or loyalty. The days when the merest whisper of "racism" would set them marching in terrifying force are past. The days of booze, cannabis and lechery are here and, by all accounts, are likely to remain.

Your TV Tonight

GPI Television Network, 8.30-10: The Doctor — the Enemy in our Midst? Brilliant award-winning Neville Dreadberg, GPI's star producer, presents a new documentary which faces unflinchingly the lessons of the Shipman case, with its latest provisional count of more than 45,000 victims.

Dreadberg's argument, presented squarely in stark, uncompromising, in-yer-face style, is that the trust many of us still have in doctors is a relic of outmoded traditions of deference, privilege and elitism, and should have no place in our modern, informed democracy. The programme offers fascinating sidelights on the best ways of humiliating your GP and making him howl for mercy on his surgery floor.

Festival

The dormant Hammer Film Company has been bought, appropriately enough, by a consortium headed by Charles Saatchi. This may raise false hopes for a revival of Piledriver Films, which, under its gifted director, Brian Hohenzollern, featured the horrific adventures of the mad philosopher Professor Wittgenstein, and were regularly reviewed in this column.

All this ended in 1980, when Wittgenstein was declared a tutelary columnar hero and Piledriver closed down. Since then, fans have had to be content with the annual Piledriver Film Festival, sponsored by Soup Hales Arts, at the old Odium Cinema in Gnomesall Heath Broadway. But the 1999 festival may well be the last.

Many of the actors, such as Bruce Braganza, who played Wittgenstein, Shirley Wittelsbach, who played his beautiful, violet-eyed girl assistant, and Sean Abdul Hamid, famous as the swarm of poisonous asteroids in *Wittgenstein and the Purple Nebula*, attended, mingling with the throng of aged and even positively moribund fans.

Many of the fans know the repertoire by heart and love to argue about whether the deadly three-piece suite in *The Furniture Depository from Outer Space* is the same as that which appeared in the parlour of the evil

Transylvanian innkeeper in *Wittgenstein and the Curse of the Environmental Zombies.*

As it happened, one of these arguments broke out during a showing of *The Haunted Shellsuit.* Normal good humour soon turned to acrimony when Piledriver's two old rival fashion advisers, Marylou Romanoff and Kay Cantacuzene, joined in and came to blows and hair-pulling.

Each accused the other of keeping some of the best horror properties to herself, when Piledriver packed up instead of sharing them out with the others.

"What happened to that luminous Medusa wig Brian promised me?" screeched Marylou, and Kay hissed back: "Why don't you crawl back into the sarcophagus of Pharoah Blothmes III that you pinched from your poofter boyfriend Ken Plantagenet?"

When Barry Saxe-Coburg-Gotha, famous as the giant vampire Count Zeppelin, tried to create a diversion by climbing upside down from the roof of the cinema, he fell heavily to the ground.

Ambulances came screaming up the road with hordes of paramedics, counsellors, forensic experts and police marksmen: a different kind of horror film altogether.

Rebuked

My note on last year's Piledriver Film Festival at Gnomesall Heath has drawn dozens of angry letters from readers. Some are written in purple ink on scraps of wallpaper, gnawed at the edges and plentifully stained with tears, tea, coffee and temperance and alcoholic beverages.

"Your account of the alleged fracas at the Odium Cinema of that ilk," writes Mrs J.H, of Nerdley, enclosing a small phial of evil-looking, iridescent liquid, "shows you are dead ignorant of our cherished horror film values. The quarrel between Marylou Romanoff and Kay Cantacuzene was sparked off by a more serious disagreement between Piledriver's rival composers, Ted Hapsburg and Bing Karageorgevitch.

As musicians, they had a particularly hard time when Piledriver closed down in 1980 and they had to find other employment. Bing at one time worked in a Midlands factory mass-producing symphonies for the Mahler industry, and bears the unmistakable scars of that ilk.

"I was sitting in the dress circle with my 86-year-old aunt (a keen Piledriver fan), and could not help sympathising with Bing when Ted tried to elbow him off the majestic Wurlitzer organ-bench when the time came to play Ketelbey's *March Past of the Ghouls* in traditional fashion.

"That this developed into a free-for-all (incidentally, my aunt got in a good bite on Shirley Wittelsbach's neck with her treasured set of vampire teeth) was regrettable, as was the tragic denouement. But if you were more familiar with the neo-Egyptian façade of the Odium Cinema, you would not make light of Barry Saxe-Coburg-Gotha's heroic attempt to descend it in vampire fashion upside down.

"His sad end, though it added to the enjoyment of a minority of the fans, cast a shadow over the festival. But why do you maliciously state that there may be no more festivals? We have already formed a committee, sponsored by Soup Hales Arts, for a festival this summer, which the gifted producer Brian Hohenzollern himself has promised to attend.

"Why not try to get your facts right? If you are too stupid or lazy to do the necessary research, then get some more conscientious journalist to do it for you. Or you may soon face a double-ended, reinforced, copper-bottomed Pharaoh's Curse of that ilk!"

Straw

"Race", says Jack Straw, described as the Home Secretary, "is the most important part of my job." If he really believes that, it is high time he gave up the office he now disfigures and returned to his original job with the National Union of Students.

The most important part of the job of Home Secretary is the safeguarding of law and order. It is no part of it to indulge in the current morbid obsession with "race", which, in itself, has become a major threat to law and order.

One of the worst consequences of mass immigration into England is this morbid obsession, this continual picking at the hated yet fascinating scab of racial guilt, which wastes so much of our time and energy.

However lofty its origin, the doctrine of absolute racial equality in which Straw thinks he believes is as absurd and fallacious as the Nazi doctrine of absolute racial purity, and, if enforced, it may well have results no less cruel and destructive.

If Straw wants to do us all a favour before he quits his great, historic office, he should abolish the Commission for Racial Equality and all the other agencies of "institutionalized anti-racism", which employ many thousands of operatives, some, no doubt, well-meaning enough, in largely futile activities.

Then, with the race relations industry in decline, its baleful shadow lifted from the police and other services on which our lives depend, we might all stop agonising about "racism" and try to behave as decently and justly as we can towards other people, whatever their race may be. That, as the saying is, will be the day.

Crusade

Is underwater motorcycling, the glory of the British sporting scene, until it was overtaken by showier sports such as football and homosexual outing, about to make a comeback?

At a hastily summoned press conference at Underwater House, the £40 million half-submerged headquarters of the British Underwater Motorcycling Federation, Sir Sid Ballpoint, Supreme-Manager-in-Chief, struck a gurgling yet solemn note amid the sound of lapping water.

"Some years ago, to our shame, underwater motorcycling entered on a period of decline. I blame many factors: lower moral and educational standards, the threat to family values and the National Health Service, water board irregularities"— he brushed aside the weeds flapping in his face and making his words inaudible — "mass entertainment, rising crime levels, the drug menace are only a few.

"In the present national crisis, when overpaid and badly behaved footballers are threatening to overturn our society and make Britain a laughing stock among the nations, I believe that underwater motorcycling, in a new, dynamic form, can give Britain a moral lead and change the lives of every one of us for the better.

"In spite of its long association with murky waters, underwater motorcycling has always been a clean, wholesome sport. Such prestigious riders as Trevor Dimwiddie, the legendary Sunderland-born world champion, never stooped to dirty tactics, even amid the treacherous whirlpools so beloved of unscrupulous foreign teams. He never disputed referees' decisions or abused, spat on or drowned them.

"That is the spirit we mean to revive in this crusade for British sporting values. And as part of our promotional drive, I can reveal that Dimwiddie himself, now 79, will attempt to reach the North Pole underwater. If he succeeds, he will attempt to reach the South Pole.

"After that, who knows? Round the world underwater, pointing the way to a world moral revival in a very real sense? It is a time for greatness," he added after a pause, as the bursting of enormous bubbles echoed round the stupendous, many-pillared halls.

Expert Advice

Dr Llewelyn Goth-Jones, director of community medicine for the Stretchford Conurbation, welcomes official endorsement of the "morning-after" contraceptive pill, whether it is taken before or after or any time at all.

"This is another glorious slap in the face," he says, "for all the killjoys and prudes and enemies of youth and life and happiness.

"It is another giant step towards the ideal society we are trying to create, a society where everybody will be able to enjoy sex with everybody else whenever they feel like it.

"It does not mean, of course, that other contraceptive methods should be discarded. On the contrary: everybody, whatever their age, should use all available methods at all times," he shouted, cramming a big batch of assorted pills into his mouth and brandishing a handful of condoms to set an example.

Dr Goth-Jones, as well as being director of community medicine, runs a chain of contraceptive and abortion clinics right across the West Midlands. His sex advice phone-in programme, *Calling Dr Llew*, is one of the most popular on GPI Television. He is also a director of Malebolge Pharmaceuticals, a mammoth subsidiary of the global Nadir Consortium.

News from Nowhere

Ravaged by huge new roads and railways, its woods and fields grubbed up and covered with housing estates, business parks and shopping centres, the fate of Kent, once known as the "Garden of England", now part of a "Euro-region", is heartbreaking indeed.

But it stands for what is happening or going to happen to all the other counties of England.

Whether they live in Kent or not, people whose purpose is to be happy must at all costs try to enjoy this inexorable process, and forego any reactionary longings they may have.

The leaders of the Conservative-controlled Kent County Council, Sandy Bruce-Lockhart, has spoken: "We are totally committed to increasing trade, tourism and commercial activity ... it is only through a strong economy that we can fulfil those wider, quality-of-life and social objectives we all share."

Do we all share the social objectives that this supremely confident

Tory materialist takes for granted? Do we all share the "quality-of-life and social objectives" embodied in the production of more and more unnecessary goods and the incessant movement of more and more goods and people from one place to another, of ceaseless change in a universal conurbation of uproar and ugliness whose only purpose is to go on getting bigger for ever and ever?

Can we save England from such a fate? Probably not.

In many a plangent paragraph in this column from time immemorial, I have mused about a resistance movement, an alliance of "Left" and "Right"— terms that have lost all meaning in a world of people who believe in "quality-of-life and social objectives".

In my mind's eye, the symbolic figures of Arthur Scargill and some great landowner still to be named, both in their different ways lovers of England, representing all who have been and will be dispossessed and demoralised and ruined by the frenzy of commercial progress, join together to head a great march on London, a Pilgrimage of Grace for the 21st century.

There go the fine new banners of the Countryside Alliance and the beautiful old trade union banners of the Durham miners, and not far behind, humble but still glorious, the makeshift banners of Captain Ludd.

As they march through England, hundreds of thousands of all kinds rush to join them. Even ecologists and environmentalists, for all their priggish chatter, are not turned away.

Watching protectively over the marchers are the spirits of great dead Englishmen who believed in a different quality of life and different social ideas from buying and selling and manipulating money, men who, but for their common devotion to the great cause, would fall out violently with each other: Milton, Blake and Cobbett, Ruskin, Morris and Chesterton.

There too, is the great reactionary eccentric Colonel Sibthorp, the Victorian statesman, philosopher and mechanophobe, roaring indignantly above the motorway traffic.

It is not only the physical obliteration of England that they are marching against. It is the monster of Blairite modernisation, with all the loud, low-minded boasts it lives in now and all the decadence and empty misery it will end in.

Now the marchers come near to London, where nests of politicians, placemen and babblers scheme among the nightmare towers of imaginary money, twitching the strings of their worldwide web.

At the touch of human reality, will all this mad, inhuman pandemonium vanish in an instant, like an evil enchantment? Discuss.

Huzza!

Is a new chapter about to open in the romantic story of Madeleine Albright, one half of that immortal duo of world's sweethearts, Cook and Albright? Václav Havel, who vacates the Czech presidency in three years' time, has urged her to succeed him.

To us monarchists, this offers an even more exciting prospect than it must offer to the Czechs themselves. Ever since the Czech Republic was set up, we have been working for a restoration of the rightful authority in that country, the ancient Crown of Bohemia.

Here is our opportunity. When in due course, after a bloodless monarchist coup, Queen Madeleine ascends the throne, she cannot fail, with her beauty, charm and diplomatic experience, to be a popular monarch.

Belying the modern reputation of the Czech Republic as a rather boring country (it is, of course, the birthplace of that Titan of the yawn game, Antonin Bvorak), she will preside over a brilliant court. Artists, poets, musicians, arbiters of fashion will flock there.

How different from the last Queen of Bohemia, the tragic "Winter Queen", Elizabeth, oldest daughter of our own King James I, who had to flee the country when the forces of the Catholic League defeated the Bohemian Protestants at the Battle of the White Mountain (1620). She died in exile in England.

But neither this, nor being pelted with eggs by anarchist students on a recent visit to Prague, ought to deter Madeleine from her manifest duty.

Besides, if anything should go wrong, the International Community will see she is all right.

Prophet

Great was the mirth among humanist thinkers when Cardinal Giacomo Biffi, Archbishop of Bologna, spoke not long ago about the Antichrist, describing him as possibly alive in the world today, a great exponent of human and animal rights, an environmentalist and a vegetarian. But even if you think the concept of the Antichrist is a relic of ancient superstition, you still may not find this account of him altogether ridiculous.

The source of the Cardinal's remarks is a famous story, *Narration Concerning the Antichrist*, by the Russian philosopher and prophet Vladimir Solovyev, who died just 100 years ago.

In this story, the Antichrist appears as a "great spiritualist, ascetic and philanthropist". His courtesy wins all hearts. He has written a book, *The Open Path to Peace and Prosperity Throughout the World*, which has been translated into all languages.

On being proclaimed Ruler of the World — after an election without votes — he issues a manifesto ending with the following words: "Peoples of the Earth! The pledges have been fulfilled ... from this day onwards there will be upon Earth only one single central power ... international law at last has the sanction it has lacked hitherto. Henceforth no power will dare to say 'war' when I say 'peace'. Peoples of the Earth! Peace be with you!"

As far as I know, there is no obvious candidate for Antichrist at present. But isn't this all beginning to sound horribly familiar? According to tradition, the world rule of Antichrist will be hugely successful and popular. It will bring worldwide prosperity, material comfort, health and well-being.

However, again according to tradition, the moment when the Antichrist attains the summit of his power will be the moment before his headlong fall and annihilation.

The Arts! The Arts!

At a church service during the royal tour of Australia, an introit was played on the didgeridoo by an Aboriginal musician dressed only in a loincloth with a few protruding twigs and clay body paint. When he told Prince Philip that he had taught himself to play with the aid of a vacuum cleaner, the Prince remarked: "I hope it wasn't switched on."

As usual, the Prince's comment was both pertinent and helpful. Many didgeridoo players not only use the vacuum cleaner as a learning aid, but incorporate it in their recitals, believing it gives added resonance. One of these is Piers Barometjarra-Jones, the self-styled Australian Aboriginal nephew of Sir Quentin Goth-Jones, chairman of Stretchford Arts.

Piers is principal didgeridoo-player-in-residence at St Bogwena's Hospital. He wears a well-cut lounge suit, a spotted bow tie with protruding twigs and just a little clay paint on the face to show his commitment to oppressed minorities. To avoid electric shock, he wears rubber gloves. The continuous steady drone of his didgeridoo, reinforced by the buzzing and wailing of his vacuum cleaner, can be heard all over the hospital, yet another "health hazard", out of dozens suffered by staff and patients alike.

But with its enlightened arts policy — St Bogwena's also employs a conceptual-artist-in-residence, a rap-sculptor-in-residence and a dozen rock-photographers-in-residence — the Hospital Trust (chairman, Dr Ellis Goth-Jones, the arts supremo's brother) dismisses all complaints as dreary philistinism.

"We believe," he says, "that these artists — we have more than any other hospital in Britain — are doing a vital job for Britain as the new creative arts centre of the world, building bridges between the arts and the community and forging links between the community and the arts."

Committed

In Stretchford, City of Art, great events are stirring. The old City Art Gallery in Victoria Square, which developed from the Alderman Sadcake Memorial Gallery at the end of the last century, is to be divided into two. One part, which will house the collection of British art, will remain in the present building, with its imposing, if flaking, classical facade. It will be called Stretch Brit.

Stretch Mod, the city's collection of modern art, with works by the greatest creative artists of today, ranging from Homi Bhung, Hans-Dieter Zwergendorf, Tony Jumbly and Alison Obongwe to Tracey Goth-Jones, niece of the lately ennobled chairman of Stretchford Arts, Sir Quentin Goth-Jones, will be housed in a new building by the Mongolian-South African architect Van Khan, of contorted glass and aluminium panels held together with elastic bands, in the new £17 million Arts Precinct in Canal Road.

Most of the British art, based on the original Sadcake Bequest, is Victorian and representational, with many Academy paintings of Highland landscapes, rose-entwined cottages, scenes of battle and mediaeval chivalry and rural families grouped with dogs, deer and other appealing animals. The newly appointed curator, Hamish Dreadberg, brother of the brilliant television director, novelist, dramatist, composer and self-publicist Neville Dreadberg, has already announced his policy.

"We shall use this ghastly rubbish to educate the public by labelling all the pictures with appropriate historical notes. Thus the landscapes will be explained by reference to oppressive landowners; the historical scenes will be accompanied by notes on British colonialism, the slave trade, exploitation of the Third World and other crimes against humanity. Scenes of rural life will illustrate the subjection of women and the evils of homophobia; and animal paintings will indicate the absence of animal rights, in those days.

"So, hopefully, good will come out of evil, as visitors to Stretch Brit — and, let's face it, most of them will be dreary old philistine pensioners with rhinitis sheltering from the rain — will gradually absorb — perhaps without realising it, who cares about them anyhow? — acceptable contemporary attitudes and ideals, and become decent citizens of modern Britain."

Howard Dreadberg, another member of this gifted family, is tipped as the first curator of Stretch Mod. "I shall make it a vibrant, in-yer-face assertion of youth, hope, fun, modernity, human rights and One World values," he says. But he may face a serious crisis at the very outset of his reign.

Jon Ghasbin (formerly John Gasby), the Nerdley-born neo-aggressivist-destructionist sculptor, has put in a forceful claim for including one of his major works in Stretch Mod. In spite of opposition, he means to assert his claim at the glittering opening party in the summer, when thousands of arts celebrities will attend.

Ghasbin's works do not wait, as the works of lesser aggressivists do, for people to approach them before going on the attack. As the critic Victor Moronowicz has said, "they come out fighting, bald-headed, with no punches pulled and no holds barred".

The gigantic sculpture Rubbish Dump XI, which Ghasbin has promised for the new gallery, will be timed to explode as soon as the full crowd of glittering celebrities has mustered. It should destroy building and guests together in "a complex assertion of sporadist but essentially neo-diagonal, yet tautly controlled and organised multi-dimensional commitment" (Andrew Sheep-Harris, *The Art of Jon Ghasbin*, Viper and Bugloss, £695).

Nerdley Man

By next April, the Chancellor predicts, tax for the "average family" will be at its lowest since 1972. But sceptical people have worked out that this will apply only if the average family does not own a car, has no mortgage and does not smoke or pay council tax or VAT.

Such families, sarcastically described by a Conservative MP as "dysfunctional", are quite common in Nerdley. Hence the term "Nerdley Man" for the typical head of such a family. Stanley Nobes, 45, of Mandelson Way, claims to be the original Nerdley Man. He is employed as a part-time turntable underlooker at a local factory, but often fails to draw his pay because he thinks it might be taxed.

"My wife and I — we have no kids, of course — don't go out of the house if we can help it. If we did that sort of thing, we might spend money and so get indirectly involved in paying tax. We eat very little and drink just an occasional glass of warm water on Saturday evenings.

"We have nothing to talk about and spend a lot of time staring out of the window. We play an occasional game of noughts-and-crosses, which does not need any equipment that might involve VAT. We have a TV, but don't watch it because I believe it uses up electricity, though I may be wrong there.

"What's that you say? Sounds a boring sort of life? Well, it suits us and thousands like us. We're proud to be Nerdley Men and Nerdley Women. Yes, we vote Labour.

"You see, we think the Chancellor will find ways of making sure that average families like ours pay even less tax than we do now. If we stick to our chosen way of life, we know he won't let us down."

At Marxmount

Meanwhile, back in the real world, there is trouble at Marxmount, Mrs Dutt-Pauker's fine white mansion on the edge of Hampstead Heath.

The great Hampstead thinker has been forthright in maintaining that everybody, whatever their race or origin, should have the right to enter or leave this country whenever they wish.

In many an eloquent letter to the press she has extolled the wealth of cultural riches that Albanians, Kurds, Somalis, gipsies and other unfortunate people are bringing to this country, just as successive waves of immigrants did in the past.

So when her daughter Deirdre collected a band of Romanian gipsies in Dover and brought them to Marxmount, she had a good chance of putting her principles into practice.

Looking up from her desk in her capacious study, where she was busy on another letter to the press about the refugees, she was amazed to see through the tall windows several headscarved women, carrying what looked like babies, strolling about the cedared lawns and tramping over the parterres so carefully tended by MacKenzie, her head gardener! And there, smiling rather foolishly as she tried to address them in some vaguely recalled Latin words, was Deirdre herself! Seeing her mother, she waved, and all the gipsy women waved too! Some brandished their babies.

"What is the meaning of this, Deirdre?" said the chatelaine of Marxmount in a terrible, cold voice, as she came storming out into the garden.

"But, Mummy, I thought you'd be pleased. These are refugees wanting asylum. This is Magda, Mummy, this is Elena, this is . . ."

"Deirdre, how many times must I ask you not to meddle with things you can't possibly understand? Go and ring the police, and have these people removed immediately! It's a matter of principle. Can't you see that, if we take these people in now, we may get white, colonialist, racist exploiters from Zimbabwe coming and asking for asylum as well? How could I ever face my old friend Bob Mugabe again?"

"Yes, Mummy."

History

Brooding on the case of David Irving, I found myself admiring (it is not yet illegal, I think, to say this) his prodigious self-confidence and his heroic folly. He must have known perfectly well from the outset that he could not win his case against such odds. It would have been to defy one of the most powerful of contemporary taboos.

However villainous Irving may be, his villainy is not the issue here. The issue is the right of historians to examine and interpret all those innumerable events that have come to be known collectively as "the Holocaust" as freely as they would examine and interpret any other historical events; that is, the right of historians, including Irving, to carry out historical research and publish the results, without being tied to a foregone conclusion.

Moreover, however unacceptable Irving's opinions may be, it is a strange sort of country that can consign him to outer darkness while conferring the Order of Merit on another historian, the Marxist Eric Hobsbawm, an only partly and unwillingly repentant apologist for the Soviet Union, a system of tyranny whose victims far outnumbered those of Nazi Germany.

Correspondence

Sir — Am I alone in wondering why so much sympathy is being wasted on the so-called white farmers of Zimbabwe?

Surely most of us must be aware that one of the principal crops these farmers produce is tobacco, directly responsible for bringing misery, sickness and death to millions of people throughout the world?

If these latter-day merchants of death are forced to stop growing their deadly crop, that will be a real boon for humanity.

As for their black workers, if they become unemployed and even have to go short of food, I am sure that the majority of them will cheerfully bear these trials, knowing that, in the long run, they are all for the common good.

If these tobacco farmers come to Britain, we should give them a cool reception and, considering the nature of their evil trade, treat them with the contempt they deserve. First things first.

Incidentally, I am sure that one of the most powerful reasons for Mugabe's antipathy towards these people must be his righteous hatred of smoking.

BRIAN GUMBS,
Reader in Non-smoking Studies, Soup Hales University

Brain Drain

Can smoking cause impotence? Dr Ron Hardware and his dedicated team of research scientists at Nerdley University are convinced that it does.

"This is the big one," he says. "It is the missing piece in the smoking jigsaw. Once we have cracked this one, we shall be within reach of our ultimate goal: a Grand Unified Field Theory of Smoking-related Disease.

"We have already shown that there is a positive correlation between smoking and most diseases, as well as social maladies such as racism, alcoholism, road rage, foxhunting, elitism and many other scourges of humankind.

"In investigating the undoubted link between smoking and impotence, we are up against the difficulty of finding enough subjects for laboratory experiment. It is a terrible indictment of the low regard in which science is held in this country that so few volunteers for research ever come forward.

"No wonder Britain is rapidly becoming the laughing stock of the world, with British scientists the victims of tittering, jeering and derisive pointing at international conferences. It is high time a government that claims to believe in science took a hand.

"Our own laboratories in Nerdley are crying out for modernisation. We need at least 10 times our present staff. A generously funded crash programme of research is essential — now!

"Without it, we are doomed to work in a leaking brain drain leading to mediaeval darkness."

Hearts in Tune

The Government is to remove unnecessary restrictions that cause thousands of children who might be adopted to remain in care. Rules laid down by local authorities prevent couples from adoption because they are overweight or of the "wrong" race or age.

There is jubilation in Nerdley, famous as "the adoption capital of the West Midlands", where attempts by "busybody officials" to prevent adoption, particularly on the ground of age, are much resented.

One typical would-be adopter, Mrs Karen Numbs, 54, who keeps a novelty shop in Kandahar Road, says she is "thrilled to bits that my heart's desire may soon be fulfilled".

"I've had my eye on several candidates for adoption for a long time. I'd like to adopt all of them. They are all very nice old people. But I think my favourite is an old Indian gentleman who comes into my shop occasionally to buy such things as joke flypaper, brass ashtrays or novelty thimbles.

"He may sound a bit eccentric, but he arrives in a big chauffeur-driven car and must be very well off, because he buys dozens of things at a time.

"The other day, he bought three tons of flypaper. I feel it's his way of showing that he needs a loving adoptive parent to look after him.

"I am making inquiries to find out how much money he has and, as soon as I'm satisfied that all is above board, I shall start the adoption procedure and set my feet firmly on the road to happiness."

Mrs Numbs is only one of thousands of warm-hearted Nerdley folk who are anxious to adopt well-off old people. They have long felt an "aching gap" in their lives that may now be healed at last.

Boon

Is the race relations industry nearing its ultimate triumph? From small beginnings 50 years ago, when a Discrimination Tester Grade III — how quaint and laughable it seems now! — might take a black man into a pub in Wolverhampton in the hope that the landlord would refuse to serve him, it soon gained the proud title of "Britain's No 1 economic growth-point", employing thousands, then hundreds of thousands, of workers.

Today, with its watchword of "anti-racism", the industry has become one of the most powerful influences in our society. It pervades our daily lives, strives to shape our intimate thoughts, dominates education and social work and is now moulding the police, the Armed Forces and other essential services to conform with its demands.

All this is the more remarkable when you consider that "racism" itself, the master key to the industry's amazing progress, is a bogus term of recent coinage which no sensible person should ever use except between inverted commas. The great Australian philosopher David Stove (1927-94) has shown how the term "racism" gradually came to supersede comparatively neutral terms such as "racial antipathy" and "racial prejudice" and acquired a conveniently evil aura of immense potency.

This has enabled the race relations industry to promote the idea — essential for its success — that the commonsense, practical belief, once generally held by normal people, in what are unmistakable facts — not so much the superiority or inferiority, but the obvious differences in the average capacities of different races — is not only false but morally wrong.

To have got normal people to believe this plain absurdity is a prodigious victory for the Lie over the Truth. But still the insatiable race relations industry seeks to expand the boundaries and refine the terms of its dogmatic power.

A magnificently preposterous article by John Grieve, director of the Metropolitan Police's Racial Task Force, contained a fine example of this insidious process — a new dogma: "Passive non-racism is no longer acceptable."

The new technical term, "passive non-racism", which seems to be derived by analogy from another bogus concept, "passive smoking", is intended to corral all those people not already convicted of "institutional racism", "unwitting racism", "unconscious racism" or one of their many variants into their very last refuge. It convicts even the blind, deaf and paralysed, who may have no means of telling one race from another. It convicts people who have never thought about "race" at all, and those

who are so sick of being lectured about it that they will admit to anything
to be left in peace.

Will "passive non-racism" prove to be the so-called "missing force"
that the theorists of higher race relations have long postulated in their
quest for a "Grand unified field theory of racism", which will show that
"racism" is present in every particle of the universe, including black holes?
And will the race relations industry, its cosmic mission fulfilled, then
wither away? I fear not.

A Proud Boast

British motorists, says a report from Gallup International, are the greatest exponents of road rage in Europe. In a percentage table, Britain scores
a fine 80.4 per cent of motorists who have been involved in road rage
incidents: once- haughty Spain can show only a moderate 64.3 per cent;
while goody-goody Switzerland, as you might expect, is bottom of the
table with a contemptible 59.6 per cent.

Britain was the first country to recognise the sociological importance
of road rage when Royston Cylinder, a member of the Supreme Army
Council of J Bonington Jagworth's Motorists' Liberation Front, was appointed visiting professor of road rage studies at Nerdley University last
year.

Dr Cylinder is a Marxist fundamentalist who wears socialist bicycle-
clips and NHS steel-rimmed spectacles of traditional design and carries
the complete philological works of J Stalin in the glove compartment of
his Boggs SuperYobbo.

He has been involved in 2,832 road rage incidents this year, has won
2,801, lost 29 and drawn two. With a complex scar pattern superimposed
on a face already deeply entrenched with lines of Hegelian dialectic, he
stands out as a wonder and a portent for Britain in the 21st century.

He believes that road rage, though riddled with inherent contradic-
tions, is essentially an expression of the motorist's struggle in the crisis
of 21st-century automobilism. In this he differs from his MLF colleague,
the Rev John Goodwheel, chaplain-general to the Front and known to
millions as the "Apostle of the Motorways". Goodwheel believes that
road rage at its highest can be a form of prayer, an expression of motoring spirituality. "We may feel spiritual compassion for the slow, cautious, rage-inducing driver even as we crowd him into the ditch in a very
real sense," he says.

Melancholy Goals

"Her taste in music and the theatre may have been bleak (Beckett was a favourite), but she also loved Manchester United — hardly a melancholic's choice" (from an account of the late playwright Sara Kane). But what football club would be a good choice for a melancholic?

There is one club, famous in its day for sheer, hopeless incompetence, relegated even from the Sixth Division and now living a ghostly half-life in what the Football Association's Department of Dogmatic Theology classifies controversially as "virtual limbo".

That club is, of course, Stretchford United, now limited to playing occasional games with teams of quadriplegics, which it usually loses by a wide margin. Still based at the old Effluent Road ground, now a waste of marsh grass amid the ruined, burned out stands, it still has a few fans, all melancholics.

They turn out on Saturday afternoons, wherein it seemeth always November afternoon, to watch Albert Rasp, the legendary goal-conceding goalkeeper, staring into his boots, having previously removed them for that purpose: or Ron Barmitage, the striker with "learning difficulties", who is easily distracted by the offer of a game of noughts and crosses.

It is a shadowy scene, haunted by memories of past failures, of futile attempts by Kevin Himmler, the former SS manager who was brought over at vast expense from the German Democratic Republic to instil a little keenness and discipline. Despairing, he drowned himself in the nearby River Stretch, claimed to be the most heavily polluted in Europe, on whose dismal bank his tomb can still be seen.

In its heyday, Stretchford United was at least pre-eminent in one thing: the high quality of hooligans whose non-stop taunting of the "Deckchairmen", with chants of an obscenity remarkable even in these circles, put them in a class of their own. Their exchange of missiles with visiting fans reached a high level of technical achievement. Just before the final rot set in, they had developed a "Roman army-type" ballista capable of throwing a piano stuffed with poisoned potato crisps more than 300 yards.

The club is kept in being by a modest grant from Stretchford Arts (Mime Division). It is thanks to this that the remaining fans can still hang about the ground, imagining, with a faint masochistic pleasure, that they can still hear the demented yelling of long-dead hooligans, the crackle of flames amid the stands, the surge of murky water from the breached canal feeder by the ruined dog food factory.

Even this melancholy pleasure may soon be gone. Albert Rasp himself, (his world record of 495,672 goals conceded is now surely beyond any conceivable challenge), talks of marrying his 79-year-old sweetheart Joan Yell, formerly manageress of the derelict cafeteria in lovely, sex maniac-haunted Sadcake Park, and running a small second-hand bootlace shop.

To crown it all, Stretchford Sports Council is applying for a £500 million grant from the lottery to take over the Effluent Road ground and turn it into a glittering People's Theme Park and National Centre of Football Excellence, with a five-star hotel, businessmen's conference and video porn facilities, mass striperama and all. What will melancholy football fans do then?

A Word of Sense

The European Football Championship, "Euro 2000", begins this week, and there are elaborate plans to frustrate the desire of hooligans to enjoy it to the full in their own violent way. The authorities have files on about 5,000 of these hooligans, of whom 500 are rated "Category C", the dreaded elite who plan, organise and direct the violence.

A Military Correspondent writes: "If the hooligans, when fully operational, can muster 5,000 men, roughly a division, but have as many as 500 organisers or staff officers on their strength, they are obviously top heavy in a military sense, with far too many "deskwallahs" and "bumf war specialists" to be fully effective.

"Not much is known about the staff organisation. But I presume they have the usual branches: Operations, Intelligence, Signals, "Ack and Quack", Medical, Education, Welfare, Camouflage, Chemical Warfare and so on. Many of their staff officers, of course, take part in frontline operations, bashing the enemy with the best. But I'm afraid there must be quite a few who spend their time at HQ, filling in forms and shuffling papers, with loss of morale and tendency to run to fat."

Stretchford was the first university to appoint a Professor of Football Hooligan Studies to research these matters five years back. Today most universities, except toff-infested ones such as Oxford and Cambridge, have rapidly expanding faculties in this important academic discipline.

Their influence on what is sometimes called "the real world" is growing. According to one expert, "The laddish Fat Les version of Jerusalem has been embraced as England's anthem in the hope that it will help provide young male fans with an attractive and positive alternative to hooliganism."

Well, perhaps. But it would be unwise to count on it. Another expert says plaintively: "People have got to decide which is more important: the football or the fighting." It is obvious that they have already decided: it is the fighting. If only the fighting were more efficiently organised, the football, with its horrible, overpaid players and its modish, drooling aficionados, of whom mob-grovelling politicians are the most pathetic and contemptible — the whole gruesome industry would gradually fade away, to the relief of all sensible people.

Mystery Intruder

When Sean Binliner, 27, of no fixed address, appeared at Nerdley magistrates' court, charged with loitering on enclosed premises, he asked for 26,417 similar offences to be taken into consideration. In evidence, Det Sgt J.S. Mackenzie, 39, of Nerdley Special Branch, said he was proceeding along Inkerman Road on a routine search for certain substances when he saw the accused gesticulating wildly at a hydrant.

When questioned, the accused said: "This is the Year of the Artist. I am an artist. I make art. I shock people with my art and make them think." When he (Sgt Mackenzie) asked what he made them think about, the accused replied: "Don't you understand, you stupid copper? I am an artist, I make them think about art." He became violently abusive, and he (Sgt Mackenzie) had no alternative but to arrest him.

In court, Binliner stated several times that he was an artist and demanded to see an official of the Arts Council. Dr F. Gestaltvogel, a psychiatric consultant at Nerdley General Hospital, recommended abreactive treatment, in which the patient would be shown photographs of young contemporary British artists, accompanied (if necessary) by graduated electric shocks.

Binding Binliner over, Dr Ellis Goth-Jones, 58, the chairman, said everybody was proud of Britain's present role of world leader in the arts. But people must not take the law into their own hands by going too far. He doubted whether providing more art galleries like the Tate Modern in motorway service areas, with special facilities for the elderly, would be more than a palliative for this growing social problem.

A Model Hospital

St Bogwena's General Hospital in Nerdley has been described as "a microcosm of the virtues and defects of the National Health Service". If the Government is serious about NHS reform, it cannot do better than set up an inquiry into the working of this remarkable institution.

Of its 500 beds, an encouraging proportion are vacant at any one time, owing to a rigorous admissions policy. Most patients are admitted only if they are obviously due for a very short stay indeed. This means that there is always room for those emergency cases that we read of which, for lack of room in their own local hospitals, are rushed round the country for days on end.

Doctors, nurses and ancillary staff at St Bogwena's have an unerring sense of priorities, and are particularly keen on keeping patients in the commodious corridors rather than in cramped wards. They can thus be attended to, in the few cases where this is thought necessary, far more conveniently.

St Bogwena's nurses have made a name for themselves wherever the nursing profession is talked about with respect, even awe. A unique feature of the hospital is the work of specialised anti-discrimination squads, which implement the enlightened policies of the "hospital trust", as it is affectionately called.

As well as the anti-racist squad and the anti-sexist squad, there is the crack anti-smoking squad commanded by Sister Grimgerda Craggs, a former military policewoman discharged for excessive zeal, who spares nobody, from the humblest "terminal" pensioner to the loftiest consultant, in her never-ending search for illicit cigarettes.

Junior doctors squeal with terror at her approach and dive through doors marked "Danger. X-Ray unit operating. Keep Out." Not long ago, a distinguished elderly foreign specialist visiting the hospital complained that he had been "seized, stripped, held down and body-searched by a gang of demented ogresses". He got only a grudging apology.

The hospital consultants are of a noble bearing and dramatic, even operatic demeanour seldom found in hospitals today. Some are gifted musical amateurs, retired actors or small landowners who may drop in for an hour or two ("Something to do, don't you know") to perform complex operations, usually with fatal results, before strolling out again, with a casual wave of the hand, on their way to club, organ loft or Turkish bath.

Above all, St Bogwena's is notable for its team spirit and corporate loyalty. Members of the staff who show an inclination to leave are handed over to Dr Acula, head of the organ transplant unit, or to Dr Howard Klingsor, famous worldwide for his work on floral phantasmolgy, for experimental purposes.

There, There!

"The monarchy are (*sic*) a particularly nauseating high profile fragment of an oppressive global 'civilisation' based on the ruthless domination and exploitation of the majority of the population of the UK and the world" — a *Guardian* reader.

What the Papers Say

In a thoughtful leader, *The Feudal Times and Reactionary Herald* comments on Prince William's 18th birthday: "There are no more loyal subjects of the Crown than the staff of this organ, from the editor himself down to the humblest porter or compositor. That is why we dare venture to offer some words of advice on this happy occasion.

"There has been no lack of advice, to be sure, from the sneering levellers and foaming radicals who now dominate, indeed well nigh monopolise, the press and electro-galvanic media. They recommend that the Prince should try to live the life of an ordinary person, with a view to making himself popular with the masses and preparing himself to be a so-called 'democratic monarch' when he eventually ascends the Throne.

"They suggest that he should not be addressed in the proper form of Royal Highness, or be greeted with a proper genuflection. He should not go up to Oxford or Cambridge, but instead should attend one of the parvenu 'universities', which, we understand, have been established by the hundred all over the country for the pursuit of vulgar or banausic studies.

"Instead of serving in the Armed Forces, he should take up some form of social work or international busybodying by which he could help to promote the fashionable and pernicious fads of the moment.

"We believe, on the contrary, that the further career of Prince William could, if rightly conducted, offer a chance, certainly never to be repeated, of arresting the present decline of the monarchy, and restoring it to its true function as the ultimate safeguard of our country.

"In the past 10 years the monarchy has suffered a succession of misfortunes, mainly due to an ill-advised and potentially fatal policy of pandering to the lowest and most unthinking elements in the country. This lamentable policy reached a fearful climax when the Queen was persuaded to indulge the whims of the mob by attending the funeral service of the eccentric Princess of Wales in Westminster Abbey.

"Here was a positive catalogue of errors. There was the inexplicable failure after Earl Spencer's insolent and possibly treasonable observations on the monarchy during the service itself to have him arrested on leaving the sacred edifice and conveyed under guard to the Tower. There was the symbolic lowering of the Royal Standard over the Palace, contrary to all established custom, in obedience to popular clamour.

"It will be in the power of Prince William, if his advisers only do their duty, to bring this process of abject surrender to a halt by his example. For himself, in short, he should not yield a single inch further. When he goes up to Oxford or Cambridge, for instance, he should be treated as befits the eventual heir to the Throne, with his own tutors for his studies in genealogy and other essential subjects, and for his leisure pursuits of hunting and shooting, his own carefully chosen companions of suitable rank.

"Such measures will bring concerted screams of hate and obloquy from the disaffected. But we believe they will confirm the warm regard and loyalty for the monarchy of those, whether Peers of the Realm or decent, industrious working men who, we dare aver, still comprise the most part of our English people."

Church Times

Who will be the first woman bishop of the Church of England? Odds-on favourite in clerical circles (writes "OLD BEADLE") is the Rev Mantissa Shout, live-in partner of Dr E.W.T ("Ed") Spacely-Trellis, go-ahead Bishop of Stretchford, trustee of Tate Modern and chairman of Football Managers for a Multi-Faith Millennium and dozens of other enlightened bodies.

Mantissa first came to notice as a militant feminist deaconess. She fought hard for the ordination of women by non-stop screaming outside Lambeth Palace and staged disruption of church services all over the country.

After being ordained and shacking up with Dr Trellis, she became vicar of Nerdley, where her well-publicised ecumenical services included

Aztec sacrifice, Voodoo "alternative WI trance sessions" and Tantric Buddhist ceremonies for the young. But her habit of wearing a smart black "Muslim-type" silk headscarf at services led to a protest by Dr Mahbub Iftikharullah, chief imam of Nerdley, and several days of rioting.

Her plan is evidently to become joint bishop with Dr Trellis and succeed him on his retirement or other method of disposal. Then, who knows? Canterbury already beckons. But it will beckon in vain if the Bishop's domestic chaplain, the Rev Peter Nordwestdeutscher, has anything to do with it. In his subtle, incense-ridden, High Church brain, visions of death by slow poisoning, worthy of the worst days of the medieval Papacy, wreathe and coil in intricate patterns of malevolence.

Dumped

In the Irish Republic, two nicely contrasted representatives of the "international community", a former president of Finland and a former high official of the African National Congress, have been inspecting IRA arms dumps to check its undertaking to put its arms "verifiably beyond use".

The British Prime Minister, Tony Blair, commends this stunt as a "very substantial further step forward" in the "peace process", and the Prime Minister of the Irish Republic, Bertie Ahern, concurs in a more ambiguous way. Gerry Adams, president of Sinn Fein, says it is a "courageous and imaginative initiative" on the part of the Provisionals.

Those not in thrall to Tony or Bertie or Gerry may well be lost in wonder. Here is a nominally sovereign state which allows its territory to be used by a private army to stockpile arms designed for attacks against a neighbouring sovereign state with the tacit consent of the latter.

It follows either that the government of the Irish Republic is not master in its own house, and so is obliged to fall in with the wishes of the IRA, or that it has an understanding with the IRA (to which our own Government is privy) to help it in its campaign for a united Ireland.

Alarming as this is for the people of Great Britain, it is just as alarming for the people of the Irish Republic, if not more so. The Provisional IRA, which regards itself as the only true representative of Irish republicanism, makes no secret of its plans, not just for Northern Ireland, but for the republic as well.

What do the people of the republic think of that? Most, I suppose, want the peace they now enjoy to continue for ever. Quite a few of them are "certain regarders" ("As you know, Patrick, I have no time for violence.

But I've a certain regard for what the boys in the north are doing for the old cause").

If Sinn Fein's plans work out, "certain regarders" will become the majority. The tried and trusted method of intimidation plus explosives (for which those dumps will be most handy) will see to that.

Genomed

The white-hot cutting edge of science and technology, once celebrated by Harold Wilson, has dawned once again in a tornado of mixed metaphors, this time on a global scale. Statesmen and scientists as well as the hardworking druggists in their laboratories who are actually responsible for the "genome revolution", compete in flatulent boasting.

Richard Dawkins, the evolutionary fanatic, says the achievement makes him proud to be human. Tony Blair says he "doesn't ever want to see science limited in its inquiry" (he needn't worry, he never will). But for sheer cosmic blathering, President Clinton outdoes all rival practitioners of the higher gasbaggery.

"Today we are learning the language in which God created life. It is conceivable that our children's children will know the word 'cancer' only as a constellation of stars."

Classified and even barcoded like groceries according to their genetic make-up, and wholly at the mercy of the Total, Global, All-seeing State, some of those poor children may at least grow up to know that a constellation, as its name implies, is itself a group of stars, and that Cancer, though an undistinguished constellation, is better known as a Sign of the Zodiac.

Boon

What an unexpected boon our famous English hooligans are for the uneasy Blair dictatorship! They provide a perfect excuse for new laws restricting the movements not only of "registered" hooligans themselves, but of other selected people, too, and even banning them from leaving or entering the country.

Such laws, as Lord Tebbit has pointed out, belong to the apparatus of a police state. And along with all the other measures of creeping socialism enacted almost daily, they will ensure that a socialist police state is what we shall find ourselves living in, without realising it until too late.

Football hooligans, with their Union flags and St George banners and other patriotic symbols, as well as their violent, xenophobic behaviour, are a particular boon to the Blairites, who can discredit that decent, traditional patriotism they hate so much by pretending that "yobs" and "thugs" are the only people who still profess it.

How neatly all this fits the grand design of the Blairites: to abolish England — or anything recognisable as England — and lead us unresisting into their new, cosmopolitan, multicultural utopia!

Lessons for Life

The headmaster of a comprehensive school devised a scheme by which children whose parents cut down on smoking, drinking and satellite television watching in order to buy them laptop computers would be taught separately from the computerless and more intensively. "Which is worth more," he asked, "five or more GCSEs or the cost of 40 cigarettes a week? Excellent ICT skills or the cost of four pints of beer a week?"

The parents did not much care for this scheme. But none of them seems to have grasped its full enormity, or realised that even a single cigarette or pint of beer is worth more on the human scale than all the laptop computers in the world.

It is no accident that Tony Blair believes every schoolchild in the country, even the youngest, should have a laptop. An alternative scheme would be to provide every child with 40 cigarettes and four pints of beer a week.

Children who did not want to smoke the cigarettes or drink the beer could always sell them. They might thus acquire those admired entrepreneurial skills, more useful than GCSEs in the adult world, that have made some fairly average people billionaires and even won them a place at the court of Tony Blair.

Holding On

A week in Westmorland, though only 200 miles or so from London, is enough to make one believe that what is called "the countryside" still survives as something more than a mere catchword in political argument. Here there is still great natural beauty. Here there are still people who keep their sanity and decent manners, unmistakably English people, and of the best old sort.

It is a wonder that they still hold on. Like everyone else, they are exposed to all the vile metropolitan influences television brings into our lives. Though they are as far from big cities as it is possible to be in this small country, nihilistic urban criminality is ever peering and squinting through their windows, seeking what it may devour.

The infamous tourist and "leisure" industries are busy exploiting natural beauty and history and turning it all into a hollow, garish PR show. They have even dug out of the mists of the dark ages an obscure Celtic kingdom and made it into a people's "adventure experience", with all its mystery processed, vulgarised and dead.

The brown signposts of the heritage industry are continually breeding by the roadsides, systematically guiding their victims into remaining nooks and corners they might otherwise have discovered for themselves. By the shore of Ullswater a signpost reads "Footpath to seldom seen Glencoyne". It is part of a relentless drive to make sure that every last solitary place is visited more and more often, and seen by more and more lustreless eyes.

Nature Diary

By "*Redshank*"

"Snow in July, we'll have sunshine forbye," is an old adage still heard in gunroom and four ale bar in our part of the country. Another old saying, "relevant", as the country folk say, to the present unusual summer, is, "Nature diarists make their own weather", already proved true a hundred times over.

As well as snow, we have had a freak sandstorm which deposited outsize date stones from North Africa on my croquet lawn; earth tremors which brought down a grandfather clock in the Chequers Inn on top of Old Frank, the landlord, causing much hilarity; and, to crown all, barn owls roosting together with a whole flock of magpies in Paxman's Oak.

And — another sign of an unusual summer — when Old Seth the Waspkeeper, last of a dying breed, began his yearly "telling the wasps" according to immemorial custom, covering all the latest divorces, seductions, rapes, muggings and drug-peddling cases in the village, the cantankerous creatures would not listen, buzzing round in circles with a monotonous droning sound and giving every sign of cynical boredom.

Another View

A new film about the American War of Independence portrays the British as brutal sadists. Critics ask why the Hollywood film industry consistently shows the British as villains. A recent article in *The Feudal Times and Reactionary Herald* casts new light on this subject:

"Such slanders cannot be ascribed merely to the demands of the 'box office'. Is it not possible that the deliberate misrepresentation of the campaign against the disloyal colonists 200 years ago is due in some part to a growing fear among the present rulers of North America and their lackeys in the moving picture industry that their subjects of today may at last come to realise that their ancestors were grossly misled in their rebellion?

"Informants in the so-called United States tell us that more and more of the colonists, belatedly aware of the false and illusory course on which they have been embarked so long, are now anxious to end it and renew their allegiance to the Crown, thus restoring their large and prosperous territories to the welcoming embrace of the British Empire.

"Should that happy event come about, all mankind would surely rejoice. The Empire, rejuvenated and strengthened by so many energetic and enterprising new subjects, would become invincible.

"Moreover — a lesser but still inestimable boon for mankind — the former colonists, indignant at being so wickedly deceived by the evil and perfidious film magnates of Hollywood, might well turn on that place of iniquity and level it with the ground."

Food Battles

"Madonna", an actress, claims to have attended a dinner party with the Prince of Wales as host, in which he was "very relaxed at table, throwing the salad around and stuff, and flinging lettuces willy nilly".

Dr Lionel Numbs, lecturer in food-throwing studies at the University of Gnomesall Heath, comments: "People used to traditional food-throwing who have failed to keep up with the times may be surprised at the present vogue for vegetarian or 'organic' food-throwing, particularly in such distinguished circles.

"They will wonder how people who have enjoyed hurling joints of beef, chicken casserole, ratatouille or even the humble custard pie or cream bun at each other can reconcile themselves to the tame pleasures of lettuce or cucumber throwing. What would the anonymous author of that classic manual *When the Food Began to Fly* think of such decadence?

"Well, I myself find that when I am hit full in the face with a fresh lettuce over the dinner table, the sense of a new refined pleasure more than makes up for the loss of the crude, gravy-sodden thrills of former days. If the lettuce is organic, the sensation can be truly spiritual, an experience of the purest, most delicate tactility imaginable."

Arts

The Government's plan to spend an extra £150 million on sport and the arts has had a cautious welcome in Stretchford. Sir Quentin Goth-Jones, chairman both of Stretchford Arts and of Stretchford Sports Council, has spoken of "the essential unity of art and sport in a democratic, anti-elitist and creative community". He said the extra money would be welcome, though it was "only a drop in the ocean of the People's yearning for art and sport as joint bridge-builders of the future".

He has already prepared an ambitious programme of artistic and sporting projects for the Conurbation which should make a considerable hole in the £150 million. Stretch Mod, the city's museum of modern art, was opened with great éclat last month, but Sir Howard Dreadberg, its gifted curator, is already demanding an extension (estimated cost, £45 million) to the original building, designed by the Mongolian-South African architect Wangdu Garfinckel.

"We need — the People need — at least three times the present space if we are to accommodate great new sculptural works which turn their vast backsides to the past and make a vibrant, in-yer-face, assertion of youth, hope, fun and human rights for the future."

One of these is Rubbish Trap IV, a new masterpiece by Jon Ghasbin (formerly John Gasby), the neo-aggressivist, destructionist sculptor whose works, unlike those of lesser aggressivists, do not just wait for people to approach them before going on the attack but beat them up straight away.

Rubbish Trap IV makes use of a complex pattern of cattlegrids, into which, Ghasbin hopes, the public will be driven, partly by their own curiosity, partly by electric cattle-prods incorporated in the "shell" of the design, until they are completely trapped, when they can be finished off with iron bars and controlled explosions. The whole work, according to the critic Andrew Sheep-Harris, is "a bold assertion of sporadist but essentially neo-rhomboidal patterns of multi-diagonal space".

Another ambitious project (estimated cost, £35 million) is the National Centre for Kids' Multicultural Football Excellence at Nerdley, with Sean Huitzilopochtli, a gifted young member of the Aztec community, tipped as first director. It will emphasise the links between football, colonialism, the slave trade, Third World debt and British oppression in Ireland.

Stretchford Arts are also considering a large grant (about £15 million) to "one of the most vital creative enterprises in the West Midlands today", the Marylou Ogreburg Bread and Marmite People's Multiracial Street Dance Theatre. The extra money will provide new equipment and improved defence weapons against the racist thugs and hooligans who try to disrupt performances.

It will also enable Marylou to achieve her long-term aim of employing the world-class Czech mime artists Vaclav and Neroda Bvorak as permanent members of her team, with a literally stunning effect on the public. The Bvoraks' fees will probably be no more than £10 million, so that the Government will still have enough left for minor projects.

Services

The Office of Fair Trading, it is reported, will enforce the break-up of two motorway service chains, Granada and Welcome Break, which between them control more than two thirds of the market. There are growing complaints about the quality and prices of the food and services they offer.

Yet the disgusting food and vulgar surroundings are essential to the service areas' charm. Like the Millennium Dome, they offer, in a restricted space, all the attractions that make Blairite Britain what it is. Unlike the Dome, they have grown gradually, and represent the hopes and ideals of several decades, their creators' dreams of what the People want.

Who that truly loves our motorways would want the service areas to be different? Who would want these palaces of mingled flashiness and squalor where a thousand jangling instruments accompany the Kids' Full English Breakfast (£3.75), to disappear, while modish palaces of minimalist good taste rose in their place?

Some of the better service areas now include agreeable dog-walks. If they must change, mightn't this show the best way forward, or rather backward? As the motorways, superseded by other forms of transport, gradually decay, become grassed over, overshadowed by a noble spread of trees, mightn't the service areas turn into finely landscaped parks, with wild and formal gardens, artificial lakes, avenues, home farms, pheasant coverts, trout streams, and at the heart of every one, a strange old rambling half-ruined folly whose original function nobody remembers?

Sneer

The Queen Mother's splendid birthday celebrations are already receding into the past, and with them, we may hope, will recede the statutory Left-wing sneer against the monarchy, fading away in muffled squeaks and grunts in the radical press on its way to the dustbin of history. If only it would stay there.

No hope of that. It will emerge from the dustbin to be recycled over and over again, with all its stale, priggish, rancorous, dull-witted arguments about equality and waste of money and anachronism; with all its boring visions of the future British Republic and its future presidents, President Elton John, the People's Creative Artist; President Richard Branson, the People's Businessman; President Mo Mowlam, the People's Landlady; President Claire Rayner, the People's Counsellor. You may think, if you try hard enough, of even worse.

They are welcome to their presidential inauguration ceremonies in the People's Dome, a combined festival of rock and rap and sex education for the Third World; a collective assertion of the equality of the best and the worst, a merging of all distinctions of sex and race and culture in a projected One World of equal slavery for all.

Another Blow

"Another Heavy Blow for Hague" was the inch-high main headline in the *Daily Defective* yesterday. In a lightning manoeuvre, Jeremy Cardhouse, the portable, all-purpose politician, former chairman of the Tories for Progress Group and now Labour MEP for Stretchford, announced that he was rejoining the Tory party. Then, without waiting to be accepted, he announced that he was resigning from it to rejoin the Labour Party.

At a hastily summoned press conference, Cardhouse stated: "By joining the Labour Party from the Tories, I am making a far greater impact on public opinion than by merely staying in the party I love. I considered joining the Liberal Democrats, as well, thus making an impact on the whole political spectrum. But enough, I sometimes think, can be enough.

"By abandoning the Tories, I have taken a firm stand against their present lurch to the Right. If it continues, I believe it will make them the party of every kind of nasty bigotry and hatred. They will end up, I believe, well to the right of the Nazis.

"We can see this most clearly and alarmingly in their attitude to the most important issue in Britain today: gay rights and full equality for the gay and lesbian communities. I am neither gay nor lesbian myself, though I have often considered 'coming out' in sympathy.

"I have something more than sympathy for these misunderstood people. I feel a deep compassion for them. I feel their pain. I am really very, very sorry for them indeed, and" — at this, a group of fantastically leather-clad militants from GayRage, who had been getting more and more restive, advanced menacingly against him, brandishing whips and iron-tipped demonstrational placards.

He managed to escape through a back window, but soon afterwards suffered an attack of his old trouble, multiple convolvulitis, and was rushed to hospital for treatment under police protection.

Referred

An educational experiment at Nerdley may revolutionise education in Britain. Ten years ago, the former Bog Lane Primary School became vacant after all the pupils had been excluded for "absolute" truancy, assaults on teachers, drug dealing and the highest rates of sub-teenage pregnancy and juvenile crime in the country.

The school was then declared a "pupil referral unit" and all the excluded pupils were referred to it. A few resourceful former teachers, mostly petty criminals in their spare time, who had excluded themselves from the school, now got themselves referred to the new unit. Now, with its unique pupil-teacher ratio and sense of common purpose, Bog Lane Pupil Referral Unit is, in its own way, an outstanding success. It is the solution, many educationalists think, to one of our most intractable social problems.

It is admirably free from either teaching or learning. It concentrates on life. No pupil or even teacher is ever excluded from it. So attractive is this school, in fact, that many students and graduates from Nerdley University, with which it has historical links, have begun to refer themselves to it. Des Biles, 56, a 37th-year sociology student whose ambitious thesis, "In the Bowels of the Welfare State", is still unfinished, is thought to be the oldest of these.

Dossing down in a capacious, comfortably furnished cupboard off number three classroom, Des is a great favourite with pupils and teachers alike, full of good advice on how to make the most of the referred life. He has recently arranged for visits from the Meals on Wheels service and has put in for special massage treatment on the NHS. "I'm dead chuffed," he says. "This is the life all right. Don't know why everybody doesn't get themselves referred."

As word gets about, they soon will.

Fated

Whether Parliament approves "therapeutic cloning" or not, will it make any difference in the long run? Whatever scientists can do, that will be done. Public opinion, at first aghast at artificial insemination and other landmarks on this infernal road, has largely come to accept them. So it is likely to be with this latest triumph.

"Science has put into our hands innumerable gifts that we can use either for good or ill." This mantra, once regularly intoned, has become less popular now that many of these gifts are plainly seen to be used for ill.

A new palliative has appeared instead: it says that we must be kept well informed about the latest scientific developments, as well as learning more about science and scientific methods, so that we can decide for ourselves whether we want these gifts or not.

But who are "we"? Would it make any difference if we said we did not want them? Would it make any difference if some scientists themselves decided they were too dangerous to proceed with? Others would somehow, somewhere, carry on the work. The progress of science and technology which has seized upon our world seems irreversible, even fated.

Will it, as in some environmentalist fantasy, gradually diminish in strength and become humanly manageable in a new, green and "sustainable" world? Or will it, as seems more likely, proceed to a catastrophic end?

Blighted Hopes

Many of the museums and other centres opened to mark the Millennium are failing because of over-estimation of the probable number of visitors. Among them are the Museum of Popular Music in Sheffield, now mercifully closed, and the Earth Centre in Doncaster, which has attracted less than half the visitors expected.

Millennial projects in the Stretchford Conurbation, all boosted as "astonishing", "fascinating" and "an unforgettable day out for all the family", have not done well either. The Aztec Centre in Nerdley (expected attendance 600,000) had 25 visitors in the first week. Most of them said they were "horrified and disgusted", particularly by the offer of "free human sacrifice for pensioners and kids".

The Museum of Underwater Motorcycling, a sport pioneered in the district by Sir Sid Ballpoint (now Lord Ballpoint of Nerdsbridge), was expected to attract at least 400,000 visitors to the Soup Hales Canal Basin. About 2,000 turned up on the first day, but an uncontrollable surge of water produced by underwater ace Ron Pitkethly had them fleeing for their lives, grimly vowing to sue for everything they could get.

The Museum of Typical Housewives' Fan Clubs at Gnomesall Heath got off to a good start, with 30,000 visitors in the first week, fascinated by what has been called "the unique, controversial tapestry of this traditional feature of Stretchford life". But the displays of iron-tipped handbags, sawn-off umbrellas, booby-trapped cakestands and finely-knitted banners with portraits of Jackie Kennedy, Saddam Hussein, Salman Rushdie and other idols, proved over-exciting.

A film of the sack of the Hanging Gardens of Babylon Hyperconsumerama by crack units of the Revisionist Our Ayatollah Khomenei Fan Club, in 1982, in which pork pie section leader R.S. Neurone was decapitated in error, was the flashpoint.

At the museum, unholy passions had been aroused, and members of several militant fan clubs soon took a hand. Within minutes the museum was reduced to ashes. "We had hoped", said a thoughtful leader in the *Stretchford Clarion*, "that the days of fan club violence were over, and that this unacceptable if picturesque scourge of Stretchford life could safely be consigned to the Dark Ages, where it belongs. Where were the police while this disgraceful outbreak of mob violence was taking place?"

Where indeed? At a hastily summoned press conference in his electronic screen-infested headquarters, Det Supt J.S. Harrogate, 47, fan club squad supremo and chairman of the local pre-Raphaelite Circle, admitted he had been "caught on the hop. It was, above all, a failure of communication." He blushed guiltily, merely toying with the plate of cold meats on his capacious desk, as Blackie, eight, the squad cat, stared steadily at him with baleful yellow eyes through dried sunflowers and peacocks' feathers in a tall magenta vase.

Enough of Che

The smouldering features of Che Guevara, with his beret and dark, tangled locks, once glared sternly yet rather pathetically from the walls of innumerable students' lodgings throughout the world. Perhaps there are a few exceptionally silly and backward students' walls where the man aptly described by Kingsley Amis as "the bloody fool of the 20th century", still presides.

Fortunately, his elaborate revolutionary blunderings about South America and Africa achieved nothing. His portrait, adapted as a vodka advertisement, is now the subject of a lawsuit by the photographer who took the original picture and regards the advertisement as a slur on the hero's memory. He should be glad that Che can promote something pleasant and useful for a change.

Mad Dog

There will be quiet chuckles and even loud guffaws in the luxurious safe houses of high IRA notabilities today and among the rank and file in their humbler homes. It is not so much the arrest of Johnny "Mad Dog" Adair that must please them all as his prominence in our "media".

For the English public, his "image", as of a super-football hooligan — bald pate, hamlike arms, "hard man's" stare, tattoos and all — will serve to make the "image" of the Ulster Protestants even more repellent than it is already. These people, so admirable in many ways, are already seen as bigoted, obstinate, boring, yet prone to violence and altogether about as unfashionable as anybody could well be. They produce very few famous pop singers, modish homosexuals, pornographers or other idols of our time.

They also have the unfashionable attributes of respectability, hard work and a tendency to stand up for themselves. With his unabashed thuggery, Adair adds the necessary element of fear and loathing to this unpleasing picture.

It is not only Irish republicans, perhaps, who welcome his prominence. He is often shown with the national flag of the United Kingdom at
his back, which helps to discredit it yet further for progressive people
and expedite the plans of those who want to abolish it.

In fact, Mr M.D. Adair and his friends (and enemies) may be a bless-
ing in disguise to the Blairite government, as it proceeds with the hidden
purpose of the "peace process": the incorporation of the Six Counties in
a united Ireland.

Hero

For all the troubles of Concorde and the dread possibility that it will
never fly again, Paul Ohm, the Edgbaston freelance technologist, is still
faithful to the good old cause.

He argues that for the sake of Britain's place among the nations and
the advance of technology, everybody ought to build his own Concorde,
striving for faster and faster supersonic flight, and not be discouraged if
he fails at first to reach it. In his all technological garden, where not a
single blade of grass is allowed to grow, he is still building his own version of the fabulous machine.

"In spite of the faint hearts," he said today "I believe I shall succeed
in my task of conveying humanity from the dark mule-tracks of the Middle Ages to the gleaming airports of the future." Quite carried away by
his own eloquence, he had not noticed the warning noises coming from
his workshop, where the nose cone of his experimental Concorde had
become disengaged from the outer atomic "suitcase" housing the recip-
rocating convolvular piston assembly.

As the dials on the nuclear tyrometer raced upwards, indicating tem-
peratures equivalent to those on the surface of the planet Jupiter, the
spluttering sounds became a roar, and there was a tremendous explosion.
For a time, fragments of tungsten, high tensile cardboard, gluton-enriched
holonium molybdenum, synthetic magma and three-ply linoleum whirled
about before hurtling to the ground.

Unperturbed, Ohm was already hurrying to his laboratory to resume
work when Cheryl Toast, the glamorous blonde former airline hostess
who has somehow attached herself to the unwilling technologist, appeared,
wearing a fetching off-white narcocryl uniform of her own design and
carrying a tray with coffee, biscuits and the latest issue of *Fly Me*
magazine.

"Go away! Can't you see I'm busy?" Ohm shouted. With tears in her eyes, Cheryl could only console herself by demonstrating, with a dazzling smile, the standard in-flight emergency procedure and announcing that champagne would be served to all passengers when the Concorde was airborne. "Idiot!" bawled Ohm. "A luta continua," he added, in a strange reversion to his anti-colonialist student days at the Nerdley Institute of Advanced Technology.

Triad

Three things to avoid: a drunken druid asleep in a ruined teashop; a pair of "co-respondent" shoes left by an English adulterer on a bench at Abererchyll Bay; a member of the Welsh Assembly in a sneezing fit — from the Grey Book of Glynsabon.

Onward

A medical research team headed by a government adviser suggests that apparently healthy people may be carriers of BSE and CJD. This supports the theories of Dr Ron Hardware, head of a dedicated team of medical research scientists at Nerdley University.

As he strives to formulate his Unified Field Theory of Health Hazards, which would establish links between smoking, drinking, "racism", Toryism, "homophobia", road rage, foxhunting, paedophilia and innumerable other ills, Dr Hardware can now add human BSE and CJD to his expanding empire.

"The implications," he says, "are more far-reaching than we now realise. Just as it was necessary to slaughter large numbers of cattle to allay public anxiety and — more important — to confirm the validity of the research, it may now be necessary to begin a large-scale cull of humans.

"We shall, of course, have shrill protests from the squeamish and sentimental, as always when scientific findings have to be put into effect for the common good.

"But I believe that, with the greater public understanding of what science is really about, all sensible people will come to accept the necessary measures.

"Unlike some of my colleagues, I don't think we should start a mass cull of humans immediately. We need to do a great deal more research, and we at Nerdley, with our wide experience, are uniquely placed for this.

"But we urgently need more resources — laboratory equipment, personnel and, above all, money. A crash programme funded by an adequate government grant, say £100 million to start with . . ."

Fair Colindale

Among the latest victims of the ravening spirit of change is the Newspaper Library at Colindale, where they are eliminating whole runs of historic newspapers and reducing them to microfilm.

Years ago, when I was researching my never-to-be-written *Life of Colonel Charles Sibthorp*, the great 19th-century philosopher, statesman and mechanophobe, I used to go to Colindale to look up the numerous references to him in the contemporary press. They were almost all derisory. A smug, progress-infatuated nation paid no heed to his warnings.

I went to Colindale by Tube, a mysterious journey, for I was never quite sure where on the periphery of London Colindale actually was. All I knew was that I emerged from the Tube into a clean, leafy suburban region that might have been anywhere. Whatever the weather elsewhere, the sun was always shining there, adding to an uneasy feeling of unreality.

The library itself, somewhere among those empty, dreamlike streets, was an unremarkable place. It had none of the attractions of the old British Museum Reading Room, with its strange underwater feeling, its lozenge-chewing refugee scholars researching the Bulgarian Exarchate, the susurration from the continually turning leaves of the great catalogues, the fluting voice of Angus Wilson from the central reservation.

At Colindale, it was simply a matter of leafing laboriously through fading old newspapers in their heavy bindings. After an hour or two, I would go out into the unreal sunlight and walk through empty streets to what seemed to be the only pub in Colindale. Then, after another stint in the library, I returned by Tube to the real world.

Even now, a vision of Colindale, sunlit and empty, can sometimes trouble my dreams. Is it still like that? Was it ever like that?

In any case, it is sad that those massive old folios, with their rich plumcake smell of the past, must give way to an odourless, humdrum collection of microfilm.

Disgusting

In a creeping article in the *Observer*, Melvyn Bragg praises the director-general of the BBC, "Greg" Dyke, comparing him with his predecessors, the stern, austere John Reith and his successor in the 1960s, chucklesome Hugh Carlton Greene, of whom Reith so rightly said, "he follows the crowd in all the disgusting manifestations of the age".

Dyke will certainly follow the crowd in all the even more disgusting manifestations of the present age. He would soon be out of a job if he tried to do otherwise. But Bragg's main reason for approving him is that he hopes to deliver the BBC from its too-numerous caste of administrators and give more power to the people who actually make the programmes.

Fifty years ago, when the BBC was still the BBC, it was often said jokingly by the even then over-numerous administrators that, if only they could just administer and broadcast no programmes at all, everything would work perfectly.

This is even truer today, when most of the people who make the programmes are devoted not only to disgusting manifestations but also to the disgusting egalitarian "Project" of New Labour.

By abolishing BBC programmes and leaving a privileged, unchanging caste of administrators to shuffle papers until they turned into paper themselves, the malign power of one of the most disgusting manifestations of the age, television itself, would be reduced for the benefit of all.

Guilt

At a seminar at Droitwich Spa, Dr Heinz Kiosk, the distinguished social psychologist and chief psychiatric adviser to the Pelmet and Curtain-Ring Authority, spoke of the future of the Notting Hill Carnival: "I think we can ignore most of the criticism of this year's event as racist and beneath contempt.

"However, it does seem that the carnival may have grown too big for its present venue. The obvious solution is to split it up and distribute it throughout the country, spreading everywhere the exuberance and high spirits that have made it so popular.

"There are still many parts of Britain, particularly in the so-called 'countryside', where the multiracial, multicultural society we are trying to build is still not firmly established. It is there, in places like Bodmin, Cromer, Penrith and, indeed, Droitwich Spa, and, of course, the National Parks, that these carnivals would do most good.

Small at first, they would soon grow into major carnivals rivalling the parent event in London in size, a key factor for social progress and racial harmony. The spirit of Notting Hill would become universal.

"Until our society works wholeheartedly to that end, it will remain a guilty society. And it is not only our society that is guilty." Chairs shrieked on the floor as his audience began a panic rush for doors and windows. Too late! Dr Kiosk, his eyes revolving rapidly in opposite directions, was already bellowing: "WE ARE ALL GUILTY!"

Plea

A spokesman for the World Dwarf-Throwing Authority has protested angrily against the exclusion of the sport from the Olympic Games in Sydney: "Once again a small, exclusive, bejewelled clique of Olympic administrators has hurled defiance in the face of fair play and equal opportunities. It is particularly shameful that no place can be found for dwarf-throwing in the very country where it originated.

"For it was in Australia, in the Outback, more than 100 years ago that this most democratic of all sports first saw the light. It was from Australia that it spread throughout the civilised world and beyond.

"Today dwarf-throwing, in spite of all efforts by killjoys and thin-lipped puritans to suppress it, has its devotees in all advanced countries. It flourishes in Britain, under the aegis of the British Board of Dwarf-Throwing Control, particularly in the Stretchford Conurbation, where dozens of clubs compete annually for the prestigious Sadcake Trophy.

"Arthur Shadbolt, the great English writer on our sport, has written in his classic autobiography, *Dwarf-Throwing My Destiny*: 'The soft, evocative thud of dwarf on mat, the high violin-scrape of chalk on scoreboard, the shouts of victory or defeat, as the long light steals through the throwing hall and in the background pigeons coo and grasshoppers chirp — all this is surely the very essence of an English summer day.'

"Above all, dwarf-throwing is a bridge between the nations and an inestimable force for world peace and prosperity. Is there a chance, even at the eleventh hour, that the haughty Olympic authorities may dismount from their high horses and put dwarf-throwing where it belongs — at the very heart of the Olympic Games?"

Next Week: Is underwater motorcycling the Cinderella of world sport?

Help

"The cornerstone of our training programme", says a Ministry of Defence spokesman on Sierra Leone, "is creating a humanitarian, responsible army". They have certainly chosen some challenging material, as the saying is.

However, there are many humanitarian and responsible people who believe our attitude to the Sierra Leone affair is mistaken. In their view the West Side Boys are simply average, high-spirited young people, disadvantaged by poverty and lack of education, whose unruly behaviour is a cry for help, compassion and understanding.

Why was their request for a passage to England in exchange for releasing the kidnapped British soldiers so insultingly turned down? All they wanted was to take degree courses here, perhaps in environmental, media or restaurant studies.

Why was no summit conference arranged, either in the jungle or in London, where representatives of the political wing of the West Side Boys and of their Supreme Army Council could have talked freely and frankly with Tony Blair, Mo Mowlam, Gerry Adams and other humanitarian, responsible people? It would have been an ideal opportunity for starting a really nice "peace process" and ending the clearly unwinnable war between the West Side Boys and Britain.

That is what humanitarian, responsible people are saying. Is it too late? Have the sinister forces of conservatism triumphed again?

Revenge

A true *Guardian* reader can detect "racism" in a haystack. One such writes to his paper about our shameful involvement in the black slave trade. Yet, he adds inconsequentially, "watching the Last Night of the Proms, I searched in vain for a black face in the orchestra and the vast audience in the Albert Hall. Alas, I found none."

Alas, he was searching in the wrong place. Whatever musical abilities the descendants of black slaves in this country may have, what they have chiefly helped to bring us are the deadly gifts of "pop music" and "youth culture". It is the slaves' revenge.

Traditional

Once again this column has felt the almost imperceptible seismic shock that denotes a move to another page of the newspaper. But as in all things, the columnar authorities' reaction was part of immemorial tradition. In the capital, the bells of the great Basilica tolled without ceasing, and the bells of all the towns and villages throughout our territory answered them.

General mobilisation was ordered. The levies of the great abbots and nobles stood to arms. In Sibthorp Square, the Prince Archbishop's body-guard paraded in their splendid uniforms, reviewed, in a moving ceremony, by the frail old prelate himself, before they left for the front, wherever that might prove to be, if anywhere.

In the countryside, the traditional panic set in. Peasant women reported signs and wonders: a waterfall flowing uphill; frogs invading a church; within an accursed grove, a brazen voice speaking in an unknown tongue from underground; the horrific apparition of a scientist, a breed long banned from our realm, busy at a crossroads with a satanic machine, said by eye witnesses to be a "nuclear accelerator".

The traditional exodus from villages and farms began. Peasants took to the dusty roads with their flocks and herds, wheeling ancient handcarts loaded with their pitiful possessions: rocking-chairs, pot-stills, barometers, string-beds, rusting trombones. The more desperate peasants made for the nearest point of the Dreaded Extra Paginal Void, only to find themselves disorientated. All were eventually calmed by white-bearded village elders, jovial millers and innkeepers and venerable organ-builders, figures of universal respect.

All this, though gratifyingly traditional, was quite unnecessary. In the 45 years of its existence, this column has passed through many such vicissitudes. But since it is at once a verbal, metaphysical and territorial entity, what is technically called its "apparent" location cannot affect its "intrinsic" location.

Wherever it may "appear" to be, even if it should be printed upside down in the *Guardian* in the midst of some banal article by Polly Toynbee, it would still remain luminously intact, in its own "space".

Territorially, the new location offers few problems of policy. To the east, beyond a forbidding mountain range, lies the august realm of Obituaries. We have no quarrel with the dead. To the south, suffused by the pure radiance of intellect, lies the minor but formidable power of Chess, a potential ally in times to come. To the north and west is the Dreaded Void, with its eternal challenge to our philosophers: is there life beyond the column?

The columnar authorities have not failed to issue their customary warning: "the integrity of our columnar homeland is, as always, our first concern. But in the event of any serious threat to the paginal balance of power, this column could not and would not stand idly by."

Correspondence

Sir — I have heard a great deal lately about the need to persuade motorists to abandon their motors in favour of public transport. But how can they be persuaded? A retired parish priest, my own motoring days are over, but my last experience of public transport — a long journey by train from Staffordshire to London — was hardly encouraging.

Of my fellow passengers (in a first-class compartment!) it would be charitable to say little. In our democratic days, unfortunately, an outright ban on such ill-mannered people travelling on the railways would be impractical and would merely make them take to their motors again.

As the time for luncheon approached, I was surprised when a rather slatternly female attendant trundled a laden trolley along the aisle, inviting passengers in a coarse, low-bred voice to partake of aerated waters, chocolate bars, boiled sweets and so on. Surely one way to persuade people to use the trains would be to bring back the civilised services I remember from journeys long ago?

Then, polite and attentive stewards would serve a three-course luncheon, not perhaps of the highest quality but at least acceptable to grown up people. After an interval, they would serve an excellent tea, with many a deferential soft-voiced "Buttered toast, sir?" and "Fruitcake, sir?" to soothe the weary traveller. As I recall, the same services were provided on some of the lines of the London Underground, notably the Inner Circle.

In due course, the amenities of a time even I can scarcely remember might be restored: attentive porters at every station, the much-lamented facilities by which one could telegraph "down the line" to order footwarmers, warm rugs, and hampers of game pie, cold meats and a bottle of good claret, all of which would be waiting without fail at the required station.

If a return to propriety and civilised habits cannot bring back

passengers to the railways and ease pressure on the roads, what will?
Aylmer Sheep-Harris
Gnomesall Priors, Staffs.

What the Papers Say

In a thoughtful leader, *The Feudal Times and Reactionary Herald* discussed complaints by MPs, particularly women, about conditions in the House of Commons: "We cannot but observe that the greater part of these complaints arises from the ill-advised measure by which women were allowed to sit in the House of Commons in the first place.

"It must now be abundantly clear that the gentler sex, which has its own special duties as wife, mother and guardian of the family, can have little of consequence to say on public affairs, save as they have to do with the present deadly assault on those duties by radical feminists and socialist harpies.

"Some women MPs — the very term is chimerical — are complaining of late night sessions and drunken behaviour. Yet we venture to assert that in those former times which some of our older readers will recall — we refer to the mid-19th century — MPs like the great Colonel Sibthorp, statesman philosopher, mechanophobe and not least, Lincolnshire landowner, were almost always drunk in the Chamber by nightfall, and thereby at their most lucid, eloquent and persuasive.

"How often did not Sibthorp at once entertain and inform the House by crowing like a cock or barking like a dog whenever some foaming radical, or lowbred bagman representing the commercial interest, got on his legs? Did he not do our venerable Parliament a signal service by rendering the ignoble spoutings of such creatures well nigh inaudible? How much better and more truly representative of the country the House of Commons would be if it had members of that calibre today!"

Feast of Clichés

Connoisseurs of the Leftist cliché at its finest and best had a real feast when Lady Gavron, vice-chairman of the Runnymede Trust, emitted a selection of her choicest thoughts.

It was all there: the modish claptrap, the fatuously correct thoughts of the unthinking. Prince Charles should have been told to marry a black woman. We don't need the Royal Family, though they are fun for tourists to look at. Anything hereditary is completely anachronistic and illogical.

The problem with the British Empire was that it was something we did to the Indians and Africans, not with them. Immigrants are constantly seen as a problem, not the huge benefit they are. Things have improved in Britain, but not if you're Stephen Lawrence's parents . . .

Left-wing journalists are fond of mocking the opinions of the supposedly stupid majority as "saloon bar talk". It is hard to imagine what anything corresponding to a humble saloon bar would be like for people as rich and exotic as the Gavrons. But if there were such a place, such is the talk you would hear in it for hours on end, and paralysingly boring it would be.

People may wonder whether Lady Gavron is a "Hampstead thinker" like Mrs Dutt-Pauker, but of a younger generation and operating on a lower intellectual level. I'm afraid that the Chatelaine of Marxmount, with her proud heritage of old English upper-class Stalinism, may well regard Lady Gavron as "really rather common".

Reckoning

A report by a parliamentary committee on the shameful and treacherous campaign against the Serbs reveals not only its military incompetence but also the persistent lying that accompanied the whole disgraceful affair.

In the first place, our politicians lied about the scale of the atrocities committed during the initial Albanian uprising in Kosovo, thereby setting off a popular outcry: "Something must be done."

They lied about the deceitful negotiations by which the Serbs were forced into a corner; they lied about the far greater number of victims indirectly produced by the bombing campaign itself; they lied about the bombing of Serb civilians; they lied about the alleged "mass graves" of Albanian victims.

Around all these lies, making them, if possible, even more repellent, floated a vaporous cloud of moralising cant projected by Blair, Cook and the rest of the New Labour gang. When the time comes for a reckoning with those people, the shameful episode of Kosovo, which now seems half-forgotten, should be a big item on the indictment.

Awareness

Dr E.W.T. Spaceley-Trellis, the go-ahead Bishop of Stretchford, has

criticised the Archbishop of Canterbury for
saying that Britain has become an "atheist"
country in which people no longer believe
in eternal life.

"What Dr Carey calls an atheist society," said Dr Trellis, "is in fact a deeply
religious society. It is concerned, not with
medieval superstitions about an imaginary
afterlife, but with the realities of our life
here and now. That is the only religion valid
for the average man and woman of today in a very real sense.

"I see that Dr Carey is to attend a racial awareness residential workshop in Sheffield. I hope it will make him realise that the essence of
religion is to oppose racism and, of course, sexism, homophobia and all
forms of discrimination. For us the racial awareness workshop is the
acceptable equivalent of the old-fashioned religious service, which it
has replaced.

"Yet it is amazing how outmoded beliefs can persist. In the racial
awareness workshops I run in my own diocese I still occasionally meet
people who ask me whether there are such workshops in the afterlife,
and whether those who fail to become racially aware in this life are doomed
to attend racial awareness workshops for all eternity?

"I must admit," said Dr Trellis with an infectious laugh, "that I'd very
much like to believe in that one myself."

Mystery Intruder

When John Grobes, 26, no fixed address, described as a self-employed
environmentalist, appeared at Nerdley magistrates court charged with
loitering on enclosed premises and assaulting the police, he asked for
39,403 similar offences to be taken into consideration.

Giving evidence, Sgt J.S. Mackenzie, 42, of Nerdley Special Branch,
said he was proceeding along Kandahar Road on the morning of the
29th, in a routine search for illegal substances, when he found accused
striking "bizarre" attitudes and talking loudly to himself. He (Sgt Mackenzie) distinguished the expressions "global warming", "ozone layer"
and "saving Planet Earth" repeated incessantly.

When he asked accused, whose breath smelt strongly of newsprint,
what he was doing, accused stated: "Why aren't you helping to deal with
the menace of global warming which, 25,000 top scientists estimate, will

turn Nerdley into a featureless desert by the year 2035?"

When he (Sgt Mackenzie) pointed out that according to a recent article in *The Police Environmental Gazette* another 25,000 top scientists
estimated that by the year 2035 Nerdley would either be a featureless
desert, the site of an immense glacier, or remain much the same as at
present, if not worse, accused gripped him by the notebook and called
him a "global warming b——d".

In court, Dr F. Gestaltvogel, a psychiatric consultant at Nerdley General Hospital, suggested that Grobes might respond well to abreactive
treatment in his clinic, where he could be shown photographs of climatologists accompanied by electric shocks of graduated voltage.

Binding Grobes over, Dr Ellis Goth-Jones, 56, the chairman, said he
yielded to none in his abhorrence of global warming and thought it should
be made illegal. At the same time, people must not take the law into their
own hands. As for the parallel of corruption in cricket, he did not think
more public library facilities for pensioners was necessarily the answer.

Medical Problem

A doctor struck off the register by the General Medical Council was said
to belong to a "tribe of wandering locums," mostly qualified overseas.
Dr John Henbane, our medical correspondent, comments:

"Wandering locums were not unknown in my early days as a junior
doctor. As I well remember, most of them were literally nomadic, and
very picturesque they were too, adding much needed variety and romance
to the otherwise humdrum routine of life in your average hospital or
local surgery.

"When times were bad and locum appointments hard to get, you might
see a whole tribe of these people, with their tents and animals — horses,
oxen, sheep, camels, llamas and even the odd elephant — encamped
near the local hospital, monotonously reciting their degrees and qualifications.

"Oto-rhino-laryngologist, first class honours, Nerdley Medical
School!" "Ulcers, peptic, gastric, miscellaneous!" "Cardio-vascular opera-
tions, money back if not satisfied!" "Brain surgeon, MD University of
South Georgia!"

When I became a GP, I was occasionally besieged in my surgery by
individual wandering locums. Some of them seemed to have no medical
qualifications whatever. I remember one who discovered I was going on

holiday and pestered me for a job for weeks, proudly displaying his own medical equipment, which comprised little more than a handsaw and a rusty sphygmomanometer. I got rid of him at last by threatening to perform a labyrinthectomy on him if he did not go away, only to find that the locum I eventually got was a necromancer with first class honours from the University of Bungrafta.

Memories

What were you doing when you heard the news of Margaret Thatcher's fall from power 10 years ago? Thousands of letters recalling that day have been pouring into this office all week. Many are gnawed at the edges and stained with traces of alcohol, tea, cocoa and other beverages. Others are written in purple copying ink on the back of fragments of wallpaper. Here are a few specimens.

"When I heard the news on the radio, I was so overcome with joy that I danced round the room, then put my head out of the window, listening to the people's cheering, which seemed to be coming from all directions at once. When the window sash fell and trapped me by the neck, I didn't even notice it!" — Jon Gumbs, 35, university lecturer, Soup Hales.

"I am a registered witch and was sticking pins in a small waxen effigy of Thatcher when I heard the news. It was a wonderful reward for all the hard work I had put in making the effigy from candle ends (thanks to Thatcher, our electricity had been cut off and we were all starving)" — Lyn Demdyke, 40, teacher, Burnley, Lancs.

"As chairman of a successful chain of toothbrush hire agencies in the West Midlands, I have every reason to be grateful to Margaret Thatcher. As everybody knows, before she became Prime Minister, there was virtually no greed, selfishness or incivility in Britain. She encouraged me to use my own greed, selfishness and incivility in squashing weaker competitors and so building up my business to its present eminence" — T. L. Grindworth, 54, company director, Stretchford.

"I am 91, but I can remember the day Mrs Thatcher was shot as if it was yesterday. I don't think they ever found out who did it, did they — was it that Peter Howseltyne, or that Nigel Whitlow or that Barry Sherman? What I do know is I wasn't sorry. She'd done enough harm, what with Suez and South Africa and the Cold War and cutting off free milk for us pensioners!" — Reg Granule, 91, pensioner, Turgis Hill, London SW48.

Correspondence

Sir — A recent case in which a couple won a claim for compensation against a fertility clinic whose treatment led to the woman having triplets instead of the two babies or even one baby she actually wanted, illustrates the low esteem in which science and technology are held in this country.

Instead of being commended, she was condemned for acting as though having a baby was like going to a supermarket or going through a mail order catalogue to order what you want and then claiming compensation if you don't get what you ordered.

Surely that is precisely what progress in fertility treatment will make possible. Future generations will take it for granted that they can order babies in whatever quantities or specifications they require. The unfortunate couple in question were merely anticipating this happy state of affairs, and were abused for their progressive attitude.

It is enough to make one despair of the future of a country where, as Mr Blair has said, distrust and even hatred of science are rife. No wonder we scientists can hardly venture out of doors unaccompanied by bodyguards, and spend most of our time cowering in our laboratories.

Only the other day, as I was working in my experimental GM plot, a mob of demonstrators dressed as radishes, carrots and potatoes, led by one dressed as a dish of vegetable curry with dhal and mango chutney, climbed over the fence and sprayed me with "organic" tomato sauce.

Paul Ohm
Atomdene, Edgbaston

Blight

Amid the stupendous emissions of verbal gases at the Hague conference, John Prescott's contribution is said to have been concerned with the issue of "carbon sinks". These are defined as "areas of forest, agricultural land or other vegetation that can absorb carbon dioxide produced by the burning of fossil fuels".

The Carbon Sink of Arden, Sherwood Carbon Sink, Savernake Carbon Sink, the Carbon Sink of Broceliande — these are a few of the ancient forests of Europe, once enchanted places, now victims of the blight of ecological and environmental management.

There are neither ogres nor witches in these carbon sinks, nor hermits nor charcoal burners, nor gold guarding dragons, nor dragon-slaying, bear-leading, sword-forging heroes able to understand the songs of birds, nor, for that matter, any birds to speak of, and those few duly classified and numbered.

This is the work of those who survey our beautiful created world with dull and lustreless eyes as though from a distance, and rename it "Planet Earth". They have carved it up methodically into graded areas of wild-life conservation, amenity areas, industrial areas, sites of special scientific interest, statutory wildernesses, eco-habitats. They have smothered it with bio-diversity action plans and heritage projects and strategic nature initiatives and buried it under mounds of acronyms.

When will the earth itself rebel against this blight?

A Great Debate

Throughout this week, the GPI Television Network is broadcasting a series of debates on the one subject everybody is continually talking about: should we or shouldn't we retain the monarchy? Do we want a hereditary monarch or an elected president as head of state? Do we, as the GPI's publicity handouts put it, want to belong to the past or the future?

Overall director of the programmes is Neville Dreadberg, brilliant dramatist, novelist, composer, philosopher and multimedia self-publicist, creator of many award-winning documentaries such as the classic *Monsters in Blue*, a searing exposure of the Metropolitan Police.

His brilliant team of debaters, speaking on all sides of the question, will include Dr E.W.T. Spacely-Trellis, go-ahead Bishop of Stretchford and author of a searing pamphlet, *Time to Go, Ma'am*; Professor Wendy Dutt-Pauker, head of the faculty of Social Sabotage and advanced demonstrational Studies at Nerdley University; Don Binliner, West Midland Republican Circle chairman; and Brigadier Sean MacGuffog, former IRA Commander on the Edgewarehamilton Front.

Defending the monarchy will be Lt General Sir Frederick ("Tiger") Nidgett, 96, veteran war hero and founder of the Royal Army Tailoring Corps; June le Briggs, 91, author of *Briony in Love* and other best-selling novels; and octogenarian James Ritchie, secretary of the Gidea Park branch of the Electro-Convulsive Therapy Patients' Association.

At a hastily summoned press conference, Sir Godfrey Fobster, chairman of GPI, said the object of the programmes was, above all, to make people think. "Needless to say, we are already getting the usual moronic bleats about alleged bias against the monarchy from reactionary Tories, foxhunting sadists, royalty-loving sycophants and out-and-out neo-Nazis. One can almost feel sorry for them."

Afoot in London

By '*Wayfarer*'

How many Londoners who think they know their city well know that in a forgotten corner of Turgis Hill, not a stone's throw from the murmuring Wandle, can be found the only remaining working oracle in Europe?

How the oracle, evidently an offshoot of the well-known oracle of Delphi, got there in the first place is a mystery hidden in an enigma lost in the immemorial mists of antiquity. But it is thought that the Pythia, the presiding priestess, and other staff of the temple of Apollo at Delphi, who were made redundant when the Emperor Theodosius closed down the oracle in the 4th century, may have made their way to Britain under cover of the chaos prevailing in the European community at that time.

A pipe-roll of 1134 refers to negotiations between the oracle and the monks of the neighbouring Turgis Abbey for "oracular pronouncements on favourable terms". Is this a key to the notorious scandal in which Abbot Stephen Warenne was accused of sorcery and condemned to do penance by immersion in the Wandle for seven days and nights?

Secure in what was then a trackless forest, the oracular staff seem to have used their ambiguous arts to keep in with the Yorkists and Lancastrians who pestered them with awkward questions during the Wars of the Roses.

But the great days of the oracle came in the Restoration period, when court gallants and their ladies would journey to Turgis Hill and ask the Pythia the most absurd questions they could think of, or add lumps of sea coal to the psychotropic vapours emitted from the hole over which she sat on her three-legged stool, or tripod.

When Dr Johnson and Boswell visited the oracle in 1767, Boswell was so taken with the exotic charms of the Pythia that he made her an improper suggestion, then, eagerly inhaling the sacred fumes, slumped unconscious to the ground. "Sir," remarked Johnson, "I fear you may suffer a matutinal hangover of a severity unusual even for you."

With a diminishing staff, the oracle carried on into Victorian times. Carlyle visited it in 1852 ("a mere fleeting mockery of Apollonian majesty which the Time Spirit hath comboguously — ha! — spewed forth"). But suburban London, with its neat villas, Chinese laundries and ink factories, was rapidly closing in. By the mid-century, the oracle was already half-ruined. Today, only two elderly priestesses, Dora and Emmeline Pythia-Jones, remain. They take turns to sit on the tripod and will answer acceptable questions with suitably harmless replies ("Time is money"; "Well, we needed the rain"). They also serve Cornish cream teas.

How to get there: No 284 bus to Turgis Grove. Proceed through Kathy's Pet Shop (decline all free offers); then through the Lord Hattersley Novelty Boutique (ditto), when the broken Doric pillars of the temple can be glimpsed behind the old South-Western Gas Board show-rooms.

Birdbath's Christmas

"And I'll tell you another thing. You aren't in that Margaret Drabble's encyclopaedia of English literature either." Mr Shuttleworth, the West Riding-born poultry farmer and part-time literary agent who is Julian Birdbath's closest neighbour, bellowed this message of Christmas cheer down the shaft of Deadwater lead mine (disused), near Bakewell,  where the doomed author sat at his rusting typewriter, working on his *Life of Stephen Spender*. At these words Amiel, his faithful pet toad and only friend, leapt on his shoulder to comfort him.

"And here's the Christmas post, for what it is." A few bits of paper floated down. There was a Christmas card from a firm of second-hand car dealers, a leaflet about housing policy from the Liberal Democrats, and a postal order for 35p from the Toadstone Press, final royalty on Birdbath's seminal work on book cookery.

The man responsible for one of the greatest feats of literary research in history, discoverer of the so-called "missing" Bronte sisters, Doreen, Sheila, Linda and Dawn, and the "missing Bronte brothers", Dwight and Wayne, bowed his ravaged head. He had not really expected, of course, to appear in Drabble's mighty work. Too many years had passed for that — years of obscurity, frustration, anguish. To his dismay, he found he was actually typing these words over his account of Spender's much-applauded speech on democracy, freedom and censorship at the Yokohama International Festival of Literature in 1978.

Reading Spender's inspiring words again, he sank into a half-dream. He was at a glittering publisher's party to launch a book unknown. Mrs Drabble herself was there and a crowd of literary figures, dead and alive, whom he had once marginally known. His dazzled eyes rested for a moment on Melvyn Bragg's gleaming teeth. Old Geoffrey Grigson barged past, snarling crossly as he snatched Birdbath's canapé. Dylan Thomas crawled between his legs.

Could that be Henry James leaning gravely against a bookcase which John Braine and Beryl Bainbridge were rocking so perilously? Horse-faced MacNeice brandished his big black notebook in Birdbath's face. Across the room he caught an enchanting smile from Doris Lessing. But a mouse leapt from her mouth and all became vague and tenebrous as he woke, chilly and bewildered.

As the faithful toad leapt onto his shoulder in sympathy, an outsize stalactite on No 2 Level fell with a tinkling crash, mingling with the howling wind and drip of water in the weird symphony of the mine.

Christmas Books

Outstanding among children's books this year is a new edition of that old favourite *The Bumper Book of Anti-Racism* (Viper and Bugloss, £12.99). There's everything here that an anti-racist kid could want (and what other kids are there?). There's a fascinating article on how to detect racism in a Christmas cake, a plum pudding and, of course, in Christmas crackers, which often have a racist, even neo-Nazi subtext.

There are hints on how to build your own race relations unit with simple, inexpensive materials obtainable from your local race relations stockist — a feast of fun for all the family, with Uncle Jim, for instance, standing in for a wicked Tory neo-Nazi, or Dad as a kindly race relations community outreach liaison officer.

The book is edited, with a foreword, by Tamsin Alibi-Jones, director of the Race Relations Industrial Council, much-loved as "Auntie Tam" on GPI children's television.

Another Christmas best seller is *Leroy Wins Out* (Wellbooks, £7.99)

by Balrog MacKenzie. Leroy Shamus Namatjarra Allende Fanon, a typical inner city lad of mixed Caribbean, Irish, Australian Aboriginal and
Chilean parentage, hears that there are racists at the South Pole and de-
cides to go and drive them out. How, after hair-raising adventures, he
eventually triumphs, securing a plum job with the United Nations, makes
a riveting tale.

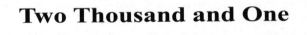

Two Thousand and One

Leak

When Edwin Goth-Jones, head of Stretchford's Leisure, Amenity and Municipal Guidance Directorate, granted Mr R.J. Viswaswami's application for a fortnight's leave to attend the great Kumbh Mela at Allahabad, he thought it was a prudent as well as a generous gesture.

Mr Viswaswami, who is an environmental officer Grade II and lives on the island in the lake in lovely sex maniac-haunted Sadcake Park, is believed to be the only naked sadhu employed in local government in this country. It seemed only right for him to take time off from his duties to celebrate with his fellow sadhus back home in the holy waters of the Ganges.

Apart from that, the sadhu keeps a close watch, by means of supernatural arts, on such matters as municipal planning policy, details of which he occasionally "leaks" to the public by the projection of "Tibetan-type" thought forms, in which he is highly skilled.

As it happens, Mr Goth-Jones has been furtively negotiating, to his own benefit, with Royal Plantagenet, a group of property developers who are planning to build a giant multi-storey car park, with hotel, golf course, conference and striperama facilities, in part of Sadcake Park, and the deal was nearing fruition.

To the relief of all concerned, Mr Viswaswami was duly seen, in a newspaper photograph, cavorting in the Ganges with his friends, and seemed to be thoroughly enjoying himself. What Mr Goth-Jones had overlooked was the sadhu's ability to be in two or more places at the same time. At that moment, giggling to himself in his grotto, he projected one of his special revelatory thought forms.

There for all to see was Mr Goth-Jones in his luxurious office, smiling fatly as he signed a secret contract with Royal Plantagenet, highly profitable to both parties; then retiring in a group, with many a wink and leer, to the more than luxurious executive suite for champagne and cigars and jokes about planning and the company of selected female staff.

Farewell

For a week this column has been in mourning for the untimely death of the man who for 10 years, faithful to the old beliefs, presided over our sister column under our primal cognomen, "Way of the World". On the day of his funeral in far-off Somerset, the deep-toned bells tolled unceasingly from the Great Basilica in the columnar capital.

In the Great Hall of Heroes (among whom Auberon Waugh is now enrolled), among the sombre tombs and banners, the abbots and nobles, bearing on their broad shoulders the dreaming loads of Church and State, gathered for a solemn farewell. The Grand Herald delivered a sonorous encomium of the virtues and talents of the dead hero.

In the country districts, too, the bells of innumerable churches tolled; grieving peasant women laid flowers at wayside shrines; sturdy yeomen staged traditional funeral games, both solemn and ribald, with rustic contests in pie-eating and ale-drinking.

On our mountainous southern border there were rumours of an incursion by bandit elements belonging to the so-called Toynbeeite sect. Angry at their buffoonery on this of all days, villagers set forth with pitchforks, scythes and sledgehammers to repel the invaders, who promptly vanished into the clouds that seem to be their natural dwelling-place

The remnants of the nomad tribesmen who once roamed the stony wastes of our then undemarcated northern frontier with their flocks and herds, brought out their ancient flintlocks and gaspipe guns; then, galloping their brindled swayback ponies wildly round in circles, discharged a fusillade worthy of old times.

Aged bards, traditionally drunk, recited praise-poems. Others took up their great war-pipes, and, with notes plangent and wild, sent out their paean of sorrow and triumph from the grim mountain defiles and stony deserts of their hearts.

A Doubtful Day

Tomorrow an official "National Holocaust Day" will be held for the first time. The "Holocaust", if anyone should need to be reminded, was not a single great event; it is the term that has been coined to describe inclusively all the events that occurred, in innumerable different times and places, in the course of the Nazis' mass murder of the Jews. Some people wonder why this day should be officially held in Britain, which took no part in those crimes. Others fear it may imply that the Jews were the sole victims of the Nazis in a war that destroyed countless millions of all races.

The BBC is covering the event in a big way, but the Government is taking no chances. Broadcasts will be under the editorial control of the Home Office, which maintains, not very convincingly, that *all* victims of "genocide" in modern times — Armenians, Cambodians, Rwandans —

will be included in an event intended to emphasise the universal compassion of the Blairite state.

Unfortunately, there is no agreement over what constitutes "genocide". Is it distinct from "ethnic cleansing"? Certainly the victims of either will make no such distinction. Shouldn't Stalin's deliberate starvation of millions in the Ukraine, and the mass slaughter of German civilians, expelled from their ancestral lands by the Red Army and its Polish and Czech auxiliaries in 1945, have a place in this catalogue of human wickedness?

Shock Horror Bid

The theft from the Foodbotham Museum at Cleckheaton, Bradford, of a historic relic of the great alderman has brought horror and foreboding to the whole city. It has also revived an old, embittered controversy.

The curator of the museum, Mr W.S. Pendlebury, 58, a full-time professional Yorkshireman, who lives on the premises, tells how he slowly woke on the night of the crime. "I heard a van draw up outside, and ponderous footsteps, then a noise of people struggling with a heavy object. I thought nothing of it at the time and went to sleep again. Next morning I noticed that the alderman's legendary false teeth, constructed of reinforced concrete, were missing.

"The thieves must have known exactly what they were after. In my opinion, it was a thoroughly professional job. I sent several dust samples, bits of old tram tickets, date stones and so on, to the police forensic. They just didn't want to know. What is happening to the police, and to moral values in general? It certainly makes you pensive," he summed up in a satisfied way.

But did the teeth ever belong to Foodbotham at all? The evidence is unconvincing. The great alderman's descendants have always repudiated them as an insult to his memory, holding that his false teeth were of a material more fitting than reinforced concrete — probably ivory or titanium.

This is borne out by the famous incident at a meeting of his own tramways and fine arts committee in October 1906, described in Marsden's standard Life (pp. 654-79). Infuriated by opposition to a proposed grant to the Tramwaymen's Brass Band Benevolent Fund, Foodbotham suddenly snatched out his teeth, top and bottom, and with an awesome gesture drove them into the solid mahogany table with such force that they remained there, quivering and jangling, for a whole three minutes, emitting, writes Marsden, "a strange, unearthly, haunting music which held the whole committee spellbound in sober certainty of waking bliss".

There is no reason, of course, why Foodbotham should not have had more than one set of false teeth. He may well have had dozens, made of variegated materials from corrugated iron to mother-of-pearl.

That's Enough

A Tory politician, the Shadow Foreign Secretary, Francis Maude, says it is "absolutely conceivable" that his party should be led by a homosexual politician. What of it? Why (apart from wishing to display a liberal tolerance or to please vote-bearing homosexuals) does he think it necessary to state the obvious?

During the past 40 years, homosexuals have emerged from a condition of obscurity and general opprobrium to one of great power and influence in our country. How has this come about? How has the personal concern of a small number of people become a nagging political obsession? The prime cause was the legalisation of homosexual acts "between consenting adults" in 1965. This was a disastrous error, not in itself but in its consequences. Homosexual acts should not have been made illegal in the first place; sexual behaviour is not the proper concern of the law.

But because an Act of Parliament had to be passed, amid spasms of liberal conscience on one side and spasms of moral indignation on the other, the whole issue, hitherto of little public interest, emerged from dark corners into flaring, shouting daylight.

Since then, the cause of homosexuality, unintentionally helped by its fascinated opponents, has gone from strength to strength. First, a "homosexual community" was invented. Soon a homosexual rights industry, parallel with the race relations and sex equality industries, began to flourish.

A special pseudo-sociological, linguistically atrocious term, "homophobia", was coined to stand for the aversion the majority will always feel for deviant sexual practices, and joined "racism" and "sexism" — equally absurd terms — as a cardinal sin in the eyes of the Left-liberal establishment and its innumerable dupes.

Homosexuality has become fashionable. It is continually touted in the "media" and the entertainment business. The more it is touted, the more it will be taken up by suggestible and would-be fashionable people, whether or not they are of homosexual inclination in the first place.

Every time a politician or public figure or "celebrity" opens his mouth on this subject, he creates more homosexuals. A period of silence, leaving room for much more important matters, would be welcome. Perhaps the permanent silence (with the necessary hypocrisy) that once prevailed would be better still.

A Model Planet

The status of Pluto, recognised since its discovery in 1930 as the outermost planet of the solar system, is threatened by American astronomers who maintain that it is not a planet at all but merely the largest of the icy bodies, called the Kuiper Belt, that orbit Neptune.

The American Dr Neil Tyson, whose astronomer's heart seems to be as warm as Pluto is reputed to be cold, explains how Pluto has changed "from the most puny planet to the King of the Kuiper Belt. I think it is happier that way," he says consolingly. But an English astronomer, Jacqueline Mitton, says "we have come to know Pluto as a planet and there is no need to downgrade it now".

The latest probe by the columnar space vehicle "Don Carlos and the Holy Alliance III" sheds a new, balmy light on this quarrel. Daguerreotypes just received from space suggest that Pluto, far from being a miserable ball of ice and rock, is a pleasant little world with many lessons to offer our own.

For such a small planet, it seems to have a remarkable variety of landscape. There are fertile valleys, mountains neither too big nor too small for symmetry, trout streams and salmon rivers, forests plentifully supplied with deer and other game, as well as wolves and bears. Towards the poles there are wild regions to attract adventurous explorers.

A hereditary class of great landowners presides over a russet-cheeked, contented peasantry toiling dutifully in the fields as their forebears have done from time immemorial, remarkable for their godly and healthy lives. Machines other than ploughshares and, interestingly, a few bicycles are nowhere to be seen. Some of the daguerreotypes, taken by electro-galvanic telescopic camera obscurer, show everyday scenes that cannot fail to move anyone who fears for the future of our own human race.

Here an aged peasant, snowy haired but still straight-backed and vigorous, sits at his cottage door in the Plutonian evening, carving wooden toys for the grandchildren clustering eagerly about his knees. Indoors, a young peasant woman, perhaps their mother, decked with quiet graces, sits by candlelight, bending her modest head over her needlework —

surely a scene as beautiful and edifying as any planet can offer.

Is astronomy, like all science, subjective? In the light of our discoveries, it does not seem to matter much whether Pluto is a proper planet or King of the Kuiper Belt.

Warning

My report of ideal conditions on the planet Pluto has drawn a scathing letter from Dr E.J. Multimer, head of the astronomy department at Nerdley University, the original "angry young astronomer" who did so much in the Seventies to discredit what he called "all that blithering silence of infinite spaces lark".

Of the discoveries of our space vehicle Don Carlos and the Holy Alliance III he asks sarcastically whether "all the planets will turn out to be the home of feudal societies where the democratic rights of the people are ruthlessly suppressed, by a hereditary ruling class of abbots and noblemen? If so, what about the asteroid Eros, now seen to be a misshapen lump of rock without a trace of feudalism in it?"

In fact, daguerreotypes transmitted from the earlier space vehicle Don Carlos and the Holy Alliance II, which approached Eros 40 years ago, suggested that it was originally an English county about the size of Middlesex, fertile and pleasant enough. Beset on all sides by motorways, airports, oil refineries, industrial estates and theme parks, the inhabitants seem to have lost heart and died out, leaving a barren, potato-shaped hulk to drift aimlessly in space, a warning to us all.

At Simpleham

It is several months now since I was last at Simpleham. Tiresome mundane affairs — turbulence in the Middle East, fears for the security of my gold hoard on the bed of an Indian river, trouble on my South American latifundia and African plantations, worries over "Europe", China and the rebel North American colonists — all these have kept me from my old home.

Meanwhile, fearful rumours have been coming from Simpleham. According to one rumour, the local authority was planning to take it over and convert it into a school of "business studies", whatever they may be. According to another rumour, a property company planned to turn it into a "theme park", where visitors could enjoy a parody of life as it is lived in a "typical country house", with my old servants brainwashed and bribed into playing ignoble parts before the gaping too many.

Another rumour suggested that a film company was to occupy Simpleham and make a film about an eccentric "aristocratic" family, the Callaghan-Jays, in particular about the madcap girlhood of Lady Jay, inventor of "U and non-U", vainly sought in marriage by all the crowned heads of Europe.

A visit to my old home was urgent. I am glad to say that I had scarcely got beyond the West Lodge before I realised that the rumours were all untrue. All was as it should be and has been from time immemorial, from the great house itself — with its mingled styles, from rambling medieval castle to Georgian symmetry — to the gardens, both wild and formal, the double lake and, beyond it, the park with its ancient trees and inviolate recesses, dreaming in the hazy June sunshine.

Thanking the servants, from Venables the butler and Mrs Craik the housekeeper downwards, for their steadfast guardianship in my absence, I took a fancy to visit Adam Broadback, the estate smith, in his random grim forge. He was still laughing delightedly over an encounter with a party of "hunt saboteurs", who had somehow stolen into the park just before a meet of the Vale of Simpleham. The ruffians soon found themselves helpless in the hands of this Herculean figure, who promptly boxed their ears, then secured them with the traditional ball and chain, before turning them loose into the world.

So all is well. What was feared lost is saved. It is as though nature herself were determined, most creditably, to assert the proper order of things.

At midnight, I strolled on the South Terrace, noting with approval the old accustomed starlight, free of the filthy glare of cities, while from a distant copse I heard again the songs of my accustomed nightingales.

Calamity

The calamity that has fallen on our country is all the worse because it means the ruin of the best people left in England, the remnant of what England used to be, the small farmers and country people who meant to raise their voices at last and to some purpose on the Countryside March.

For each one of these we could readily spare thousands of the fashionable charlatans and perverts of the entertainment industry, the rock stars and rap stars, the television personalities, the anti-discrimination operatives, social engineers, paper-shuffling bureaucrats, inflated businessmen, lying, shameless politicians and all the other parasites who flourish in a land where men decay.

The Labour government, the whole Left-liberal establishment and the "political correctness" gang certainly know their enemies. But even a certificated conspiracy theorist like myself can hardly believe that the foot and mouth epidemic is a deliberate plot to complete the destruction of the hated farmers. No such plot is necessary to achieve that end.

If, like the miners before them, the farmers and their families are ruined, dispossessed, deprived of their livelihood and given, perhaps, some insulting compensation for the inestimable loss of everything that makes them what they are, what will become of them? Will they be condemned to idleness, drugs and dole and petty crime, or to work in the unworthy tourist industry or in phantasmal "industries" such as call centres, prisoners and slaves of the all-too-well-named web?

What an epitome of a country that has lost its hold on reality and lives on illusions instead!

Rural Pursuits

Jim Yagoda, developmental and policy co-ordinator of the extremist Stretchford branch of the Ramblers' Association, yesterday addressed an estimated 40,000 ramblers on the crisis in the countryside: "It has been well said that the farmers' difficulty is the ramblers' opportunity. It is our duty to press home, with pitiless rigour, brushing aside the petty restrictions of the so-called Labour government, our eternal struggle for the right to roam.

"Now is our chance to smash, once and for all, while he is weak, our hereditary enemy the farmer, and with him the feudal landowner and all the oppressive apparatus of private property."

Later he led a picked force of "footpath freedom fighters" on an operation to liberate a disputed footpath adjoining the heavily fortified Ohm Farm, the domain of Old Seth Roentgen, Britain's most eminent agrotechnologist.

But as the expedition approached, sirens sounded, parts of the laser-operated outlying buildings seemed to dissolve in an unnerving way and a group of giant laboratory-bred hens rushed out furiously, growling and barking. The bold activists fled.

"Bain't no foot an' mouth on me!" chuckled Old Seth. "Bah goom, look you, begorah, och awa', isn't it!" he went on (he is one of the last remaining speakers of the genuine old British composite dialect) as he sat watching the closed circuit television in his nuclear-operated privy, with a big slice of Old Mother Giles's Traditional Farmhouse Currant Pasty in his hand.

Respect

After condemning the petty provincialism of London literary circles and bustling off to the United States, Salman Rushdie is reported to be back here again. This is good news for Stretchford people, who have taken a keen interest in Rushdie ever since a fatwa was pronounced against him, with a price on his head.

They are quite used to sighting him in the neighbourhood, sometimes in several places at once, instantly recognisable by his accompanying bodyguards, individual beard and prominent rolling eyes. Lately, their interest increased when some Iranian clerics declared the fatwa still valid, together with the reward.

But they are disappointed, to say the least, that no details of the price on Rushdie's head have been given. Is it subject to inflation? Will it be taxed at source, by VAT or otherwise? What is the method of payment — cheque, postal order, cash or banker's order? After all why should anyone go to all the trouble and possible expense of killing Rushdie without being sure of collecting the dosh? These are some of the questions that reflective, principled people are asking.

"There are quite a lot of things I'd like to ask that Rushdie," says Frank Elbow, 74, a typical reader who gives an address at the Lampton Road Public Library. "When his book *Pathetic Verses*, or something, was publicly burned in Bradford and there was a lot of fuss among Muslims and such, I naturally went out and bought it, thinking there'd be some real home-truths about Pakis and their nasty habits in it. But there wasn't a single word! I was disgusted.

"So, if ever I meet Rushdie on a dark night, I'm going to demand my money back — and no messing about. He wants to show a bit of respect."

Provincial News

Are the feuding housewives' clubs of Stretchford, largely quiescent since they mutually agreed to stand down under the Pact of Nerdbridge (1992), about to break out again, plunging the Conurbation into nameless dread and making daily life even more disagreeable than it would be otherwise?

To those who have studied these matters, the rise of the Taliban in far-off Afghanistan rings an unmistakable alarm bell. The Taliban seem to have all the qualities likely to appeal irresistibly to the militant housewives of Stretchford: vigour, ferocity, fanaticism, ruthless determination and total disregard of Western liberal values. That the housewives are armed with outsize, iron-tipped handbags and sawn off stubby umbrellas rather than with machine-guns and rocket launchers, makes little difference in principle.

Sure enough Mrs E. Nobes, a founder member of the once powerful Our Jackie Onassis Fan Club, now extinct, has just announced the formation of an Our Taliban Fan Club. And as though by an ineluctable law, an Anti Our Taliban Fan Club has sprung up in deadly rivalry. It cannot be long before a Revisionist Anti Our Taliban, an Environmental (Green Front) Our Taliban and innumerable others appear.

Mrs Nobes has written to the Taliban leader, Mullah Omar, pledging "our full, unconditional support in the struggle against statues and other works of art, art galleries, museums, art historians and other threats to the mental and physical wellbeing of ordinary people", but has had no reply so far. Mrs M. Rubble of the Revisionist Our Taliban, has written offering to send cakes and knitted jumpers, and sets of ornamental fire irons "which will be useful to you in your work. We are also trying to produce enriched uranium."

Is the present lull in violent operations likely to continue? Or is it, as a thoughtful leader in the *Stretchford Clarion* speculates, "a mere presage of things to come, when some new flashpoint may ignite the deadly tinderbox that is the fan club phenomenon?"

At a hastily summoned press conference, Det. Supt J.S. Harrogate, 52, the police fan club supremo and chairman of the local Pre-Raphaelite Circle, spoke of his fears for the future, while the state-of-the-art electronic wall-map winked and bleeped with the latest intelligence from the streets. "We are dealing with imponderables here," he stated, eyeing the plate of cold meat on his desk with unmistakable foreboding while Blackie, the squad cat, nine, stared at him with baleful yellow eyes through peacock feathers and dried sunflowers in a tall, strangely wrought magenta vase.

Your TV Tonight

The Tubers: GPI Network, 6.30-7: Fiona's trip to Kosovo with her porn 'n' junk mobile boutique is called off again when popular Grumbridge vets Tim and Frank Siddiqi pronounce another fatwa. Will Jon Broadcloth, mystery man, paralibrarian and self-styled one-time fighter with the Mujahaddin in Afghanistan, offer his help? Will Rex Blatters, head of the local race relations outreach (resource and cost analysis) unit, one of midwife Cheryl Breath's old admirers, intervene?

The village dramatic society plans a repeat performance of *Tess of the Nibelung*, with glamorous Pushpam Hinduja, Nagpur-born resident psychiatrist at the Old Bell, in the name part. But up at the Manor, Col Palamountain is threatening to use his Crimean War cannon to bombard the village hall with his giant extra-special, magma-hot hyper-vindaloo meatballs.

Bad Cess

At this moment, or so we are told (you can't be too sceptical where space is concerned), Russian scientists are working hard to bring their old space-vehicle Mir down in the Pacific in one piece some time next week. One of their problems is that Mir, which is shabby, degraded and held to-gether with string and chewing gum after many years in space, may col-lide with a bit of the miscellaneous detritus which innumerable space missions have left floating in orbit.

Whose universe is this supposed to be? Whoever asked technolo-gists to dump their disgusting, banausic rubbish in the once pure heav-ens? Whoever wanted their gadgets — products of childish curiosity and destructiveness? When in malignant mood, I sometimes hope that one day a big piece of malodorous rubbish may fall back on the place where all this folly originated, the Nasa headquarters in America. That would give the jabbering exultant mob of scientific inmates the fright of their lives.

Unhelpful

Will the foot and mouth epidemic affect the "safari park" of fabulous monsters which is one of the main attractions at Mountwarlock, "stately home" of the Earl of Mountwarlock in Leicestershire? The other day a party of officials and veterinary experts from the Ministry of Agriculture arrived to inspect the park and its inhabitants. They were greeted cor-dially by Phantomsby, the Earl's factotum, one of the few practising werewolves left in the Midlands.

"Make yourselves at home, gentlemen," he growled, showing his gleaming white incisors in an infectious smile. "We have no secrets here." However expert at dealing with cows, sheep, pigs and other domestic animals, these officials were at a loss with basilisks, wyverns, chimeras and gorgons. But the general opinion, particularly after one of the vets, a Mr Tim Mackenzie, approaching a gorgon too closely, had been petrified, was that all the fabulous monsters should be destroyed.

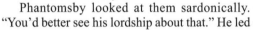

Phantomsby looked at them sardonically. "You'd better see his lordship about that." He led them to a glade, the gloomiest in all the tenebrous domains, the Earl's favourite place of resort when in vacant or in pensive mood.

He was there now — an impressive figure, eight-feet tall, dressed entirely in midnight black, with the family trait, a cyclops eye. A few drops of rain ran down his face of lichened stone. He looked as if he had been there for centuries, as perhaps he had.

The mere sight of him ought to have warned them of their peril. But the visitors, still arguing about whether the fabulous monsters should be classified as cows, pigs or sheep, began wandering about the enormous park. One was incinerated by a wyvern's fiery breath, another fell into the crater of the artificial volcano, which is operated by subterranean fires and boiling porridge. One strayed into the Visitors' Rest Centre and was trapped in the Bed of Procrastes.

Several, venturing into Circe's Boutique, were turned to swine, uneasily aware that they were themselves potential carriers of foot and mouth. By nightfall, only one remained alive. Phantomsby, who was growing ever more excited at the rising of the full moon, detained him with amiable conversation until the moment of his dreadful transformation.

With the Nodules

On a fine, early spring morning, Harry and Janet Nodule, the well-known South London traffic-jam fans, were setting off from their home in Brassgrove Park for a day's outing. "What with all these peculiar goings-on at farms," Janet said excitedly, as a sort of red patch appeared in the central part of the front of her head. "There'll be lots of sightseers, so we're bound to find a good snarl-up."

Harry was not sure, pointing out that people had been told to keep away from the country. "Oh, Harry," Janet whined. "Don't be a spoilsport.

It'll be the first snarl up of the year, a day to remember."

So they trundled off in the Boggs Snail Popular, and soon came to a farm where there seemed to be a sort of big bonfire. Janet got her camera ready. But when Harry started driving through the gates, two policemen stopped them. "Keep out. Can't you read?"

"There's no need to be rude," Janet said. "Really, you'd think they didn't want people to visit the countryside. What will become of the tourist industry, a key factor in Britain's economy? And how are we supposed to understand the farmers' plight we hear so much about if we can't see it for ourselves?"

Small drops of watery substance began to come out of the two small apertures in the top front part of Janet's head. Seeing a big man in wellies advancing on them, brandishing a spade, Harry started backing the car, which immediately got stuck in the mud. He began scratching the top part of his own head where it came to a marked point.

Shock Horror Bid

In respectable, liberal-minded, middle class company there is no more certain way of producing, according to circumstances, a gasp of horror or a pitying laugh than to say "Enoch was right". John Townend, a Yorkshire MP who is retiring from Parliament at the forthcoming election, has just had this experience, in his case a gasp of horror from William Hague.

"John Townend's remarks on immigration and asylum," Hague pronounces, "in no way reflect the position of the Conservative Party. They are totally unacceptable." He goes on to extrude the statutory verbiage welcoming "the contribution increasingly made to our society by people from the ethnic minority communities".

That is all very well. But an important part of that contribution was what Mr Townend was talking about, as Enoch Powell was talking about it 30 years ago. Of course "Enoch was right", not — as yet — in his premonition about "rivers of blood", but in his perception that mass immigration was the means by which our society would be overturned and changed utterly from what it had been for centuries.

Who can honestly deny it? It is not merely that towns and cities have been part-colonised by alien peoples; it is also that the paralysing blight of "political correctness" now lies heavily on our spirits and makes us into guilt-ridden neurotics, afraid to express our thoughts in plain language.

The fashionable view, which Mr Hague and all politicians of all the respectable parties are constrained to share, whether through staggering innocence or staggering love of votes, is that this outcome is an unquestionably good thing, and in the fullness of time, if everybody does as he is told, will lead to a multiracial paradise from which all awareness of racial differences will have been expunged.

That is the fashionable view at present, the view that all respectable people are supposed to hold, or at least to say they do. But can this view, so convenient for a cosy, easy life but so incompatible with reality, last for ever?

Is This Your Problem?

Dear Clare Howitzer,

I am 30 years old, four feet seven, slightly balding with a strong neck and shoulders, and am considered quite attractive. As a believer in sex equality, I am anxious to enlist in the Army as a frontline soldier.

I have no military experience apart from practising drill movements at home and shouting at passing cars. But in the call centre where I work I have shown that I can climb along the walls, hang out of windows, lift heavy weights, keep going on emergency rations such as other people's sandwiches and generally cope with active service conditions.

How can I set about enlisting and acquiring the Green Beret of the Commandos (or any other coloured beret available)? The staff at the sex equality awareness course I attend are not at all encouraging. Ms Trant, the head instructor, who has three Greenham Common campaign medals and two anti-Trident, says I should not serve in the Army until it is free of militarism and employed only in peacekeeping duties — Lynn Gumbs, Nerdley.

CLARE HOWITZER replies: You do not mention the most important thing about joining the Army, that as a woman you can easily get discharged and then sue for £1 million for harassment because of lesbianism, pregnancy, incompetence, etc.

As for Ms Trant, you could show your military qualities by knocking her over and then piling heavy chairs, tables and cupboards on top of her. Bring a heavy machine gun with you to show you mean business.

The Arts! The Arts!

Marylou Ogreburg, whose Bread and Marmite People's Multiracial Street Dance Theatre has blazed a trail for the creative arts through the mentally scorched earth of the West Midlands, is indignant at her meagre share of the Arts Council handouts just announced by "Chris" Smith, the Culture Minister.

"This does not reflect the vital role of street dance theatre in the cultural life of the nation," says Marylou, a tall, bony woman with lensless glasses who comes from Dissentville, Ohio, with "a mission to bring compassion and democracy to the dark, classridden recesses of Britain".

"Spread over three years, our additional grant of £2 million will provide no more than a hand-to-mouth existence. Equipment, costumes, physical and mental training, including the martial arts — all this calls for something more than reluctant charity. In modern conditions, we literally have to fight to bring the arts to people who barricade themselves in their homes and even dig elephant traps in the street to put us out of action."

Marylou's new street dance happening, Give us a Grant of £10 Million or be Shamed at the Bar of World Opinion, has been praised by the street dance critic Ian Fetch as "the real, raw stuff, of dance — a palpitating, in-yer-face statement of democratic values for our time."

Shame!

Talking of military affairs, many people must have noticed that one distinguished figure was missing from the throng of field marshals who gathered for dinner last week to raise money for the Army Benevolent Fund. He was, of course, Lt Gen Sir Frederick ("Tiger") Nidgett, founder of the Royal Army Tailoring Corps and Hero of Port Said, the man who, as he tells us in his autobiography *Up Sticks and Away*, "held the fort in the dark days of 1942 when the Nazi hordes were bellowing tastelessly, in true Teutonic fashion, at the gates of Egypt."

But, you may say, Nidgett never was a field marshal, so why should he have been present at the field marshals' dinner? That is the whole point. That Nidgett was denied promotion above the rank of Lieutenant General is, for many historians, one of the most shocking and underplayed scandals of the war. For his inspired initiatives alone, after he had "settled accounts with the Hun in North Africa", he surely deserved better of his country than bleak indifference.

As most historians agree, his plans for mass drops of exploding coat hangers (1943) and three-legged self-combusting trousers (1944) on Germany would, if implemented, have either shortened or lengthened the war. It was Air Marshal Harris who "shot down Nidgett's plans in flames," on the ground of possible civilian injuries.

"Too much lovey-dovey squeamishness," is Nidgett's comment. "Too much red tape and sheer incompetence. Above all, too much jealousy and intrigue in high places."

One retired RATC man, RSM Trousercutter Stan ("Jock") Lazarowicz, scion of a distinguished Edinburgh family, says indignantly in his personal Scots dialect: "Aye, if the Tiger had his due, he'd be Field Marshal 10 times over, wi' 10 batons an' a'. It girds me, ye ken, tae think o' a' they daft auld bauchles an' bletherin' scrimshankers i' the halls o' the mighty, guzzlin' awa' on the fruits o' the airth, and him left oot i' the cauld blast."

However, perhaps restrained by a quiet word from Nidgett himself, Lazarowicz, who is chairman of RATC Veterans against War and Military Tailors for Peace, called off his projected picketing of the field marshals' dinner, at which activist veterans were to have hurled outsize thimbles and collar stiffeners at those unjustly lighted windows.

The Tiger's own comment, barked through the letterbox of Tailoringdene, his rhododendron-encircled home near Godalming, was "no comment".

Dee Bladder's Diary

Apr 5: The most absurd thing happened to me yesterday. I was wondering where to put one of those gloriously expensive old miner's lamps I'd just bought at Bric-a-Brac, the marvellous new junk shop in Fulham, and had just decided on one of the downstairs loos, when — silly me! — I got my left foot jammed in the works and couldn't get it out.

I mean, what does one do in a case like this? Does one ring the fire brigade? Or Arthur Scargill? Or does one just put up with it and hobble along for consolation to Lars Porsena, the heavenly new Etruscan bistro (it's superlatively Now!) in Kensington, where you can tuck into a North Korean mudifish pie as good as any this side of Pyongyang?

Boon

The Macpherson Report's definition of a "racist incident" as "any incident perceived to be racist by the victim or any other person" is causing immense trouble and confusion for all concerned. Yet there is a simple answer. As I have pointed out before, the Racial Prejudometer was originally developed by the West Midland firm of Ethnicaids for use by the race relations industry, but is now available to everybody (ask your nearest race relations stockist).

Inexpensive and handy for pocket or handbag, you simply point it at any person (including yourself) you suspect of "racism", press the easy-to-find "action" button and read off the result in prejudons, the internationally recognised scientific unit of racial prejudice.

A satisfied client writes: "After reading the Macpherson Report, I began to worry about being racist. I was sleeping badly and losing my appetite. My job in an important call centre was at risk. My marriage was on the rocks.

"Then a friend told me about the prejudometer. What a difference! As I began to use it regularly, all my worries about racism vanished! Now I sleep like a baby, eat like a horse and am so full of energy and keenness that I have been promoted call centre section leader. I have just returned from an idyllic 'second honeymoon' in Florida and feel like a million dollars. Thank you, Ethnicaids, for all you have done for me." (Name and address supplied).

This is only one of thousands of testimonials. Why, then, is the prejudometer not in use by everybody in Britain today? Is it because of an all too common fear of science and technology? This simple electronic device is admittedly not yet perfect. There have been incidents in London when black people, Indians, Pakistanis, Somalis, Chinese, Japanese and others have all been involved, causing their prejudometers to "over-read" and implode.

"There are still some snags and headaches to be ironed out," says a spokesman for Ethnicaids. "But the backroom boys in our research division are working flat out, and one of these fine mornings they're going to come up with the complete answer. Then we'll all be able to think about racism not just some of the time but every minute of our lives."

Welcome

Stretchford Council's department of tourism, amenity, leisure and municipal guidance, under the dynamic leadership of Sir Edwin Goth-Jones, is going all out to attract foreign tourists to the conurbation, following Tony Blair's inspiring clarion call: "Britain is open for business."

A finely wrought brochure, illustrated in 12 colours, reads: "Ignore reports of a country where rival gangs of corrupt, greedy farmers and cold-hearted epidemiologists battle for control of a devastated land. The true heart of Britain is still beating strongly, and nowhere more than in fabled Stretchford, with its unique combination of old world charm and vibrant modern technology.

"Visit the heart of the city, with its awe-inspiring municipal tower blocks and multi-storey car parks, mingling with such ancient architectural treasures as the half-timbered National Handbag Museum, the reputed birthplace of gay rights pioneer Piers Gaveston, the Arthur Grudge Environmental Centre and the historic Stoatmarket.

"Visit lovely, sex maniac-haunted Sadcake Park, now at its most glorious in the famous West Midland Spring, where a host of delights awaits you. Walk where Robin Hood may once have walked, as well as scores of later celebrities: Shakespeare, Milton, Dante, Gladstone, Disraeli, Kafka, Garibaldi, Salman Rushdie and dozens more.

"Visit the tradition-drenched St Oick's district, named after St Oick, the 7th-century Apostle of Stretchford, celebrated for his life in a typical wall-to-wall-carpeted hermit's grotto and his defiance of the wicked King Penda of Mercia.

"Visit the Canal Road district, Stretchford's university quarter, with as many as 200 universities and its exciting "town and gown" riots, in which visitors can join for a small fee, and enjoy all the thrills and spills of life in the Dark Ages"

Symbols

A proposal to display Easter lilies in the great hall of Stormont this weekend angered Unionist members of the Assembly because the lilies are a recognised symbol of the Easter Rising of 1916 and the proclamation of the Irish Republic. So the Assembly was recalled from its recess to discuss the matter.

Nationalists and members of the Alliance Party complained that they were being made to look ridiculous. "What sort of lunacy has descended on this Assembly," said one, "that we have to be urgently recalled over a bowl of lilies?"

Another said the lilies, if allowed, would be "a first step to addressing the issue of symbols".

But the "issue of symbols" will not easily go away, either in Ireland or anywhere else. The Unionists, narrow-minded though they may seem, are right. How would we like it if the symbol of the swastika were displayed in Westminster Hall?

Spring, 2001

It is as though the smoke from the burning of the animals had settled as a heavy grey cloud over the whole of England. At times it even seems to make a mockery of spring, as nature — heartless, witless nature — goes about her customary work of growth in spite of this great crime against creation.

There is not much relief to be found in the hatred and contempt that decent people feel against the politicians and experts who preside over this mass slaughter, arguing irresolutely over the best methods of carrying it out. They lecture us on our patriotic duty to the tourist industry. Is it true that the trades of the souvenir peddler and the ice cream vendor have become the mainstays of a once great nation?

There are odious voices in the "media" which try to persuade us that the holocaust of the animals will be a good thing in the end, because it means the end of farming in England, that is, the end of farmers other than agrotechnologists, the end of some of the best men left in England, men instinctively conservative in the true sense — steady, independent and bloody-minded.

It is these very qualities that make such men hated by the present leaders of public opinion in England, those who hate England and hope to see the end of her.

A Great Teacher

Trevor Gumbs, who teaches English at Bog Lane Secondary School in Stretchford, had to retire hurriedly from the National Union of Teachers' annual conference at Cardiff when he swallowed part of a placard while heckling Mr Blunkett, the Secretary of State for Education. Rejected as an environmental health hazard by all the local hospitals, he was rushed by ambulance to St Bogwena's General Hospital in Nerdley, 120 miles away, strip-searched for cigarettes by Sister Grimgerda's anti-smoking squad, left for six hours in a corridor heaped with leftover food and then discharged.

None the worse for all this, he says he is only sorry he had to stop abusing Mr Blunkett: "One of the most sinister agents of reaction in Britain, a fungoid growth on the face of educational progress."

Trevor has always taken a prominent part in the traditional heckling of Blunkett at NUT conferences. He holds an NUT medal (first class) for conspicuous gallantry which he won at the historic conference of 1996 when Blunkett, then shadow secretary of state for education, had to take refuge in a broom cupboard. In 1998, Trevor won a bar to his medal for bawling at Blunkett louder than any other teacher. He even made horrible faces at Blunkett's guide dog, furious and frustrated at not being able to get near enough to kick it.

He is looking forward to next year's conference. "Blunkett and his fascist dog, unfortunately, may not be there. But I shall play my part in the confrontation with whoever is minister for education in a vital part of my long march through the institutions."

Count Us Out

A helpline set up for Sunday's census has been overwhelmed with calls for help. Is this due to the greater complexity of the questions in this census, compared with the last, or to the growing dimness of the people or — more encouraging — their growing resentment at state interference in their personal affairs?

On the other hand, many people are anxious, even desperate to co-operate. Some, faced with questions about marriage and divorce, are filling out their forms with long, embittered accounts of marital and testamentary disputes, usually contradicting each other ("She should never have got that barometer when Alice died", "But Dad promised it to her. It was a sacred trust").

Some of these forms are gnawed at the edges, charred or roughly torn across in the course of argument, then glued together again. Many are deeply stained with rings of tea, coffee or alcoholic beverages. But it is the questions on "race", or "ethnicity" as it is fashionably called, that are causing most of the trouble in the Stretchford Conurbation, with its record number of "ethnic minorities". Workers in the race relations industry

have given their "ethnicity" as "multiracial". Others, who describe themselves as Sumerians, want forms on clay tablets, written in cuneiform.

The Aztec community in Nerdley have refused to co-operate because
the "ethnic" categories do not include "Aztec". In a stormy meeting of
the race relations outreach committee of Nerdley council, Councillor J.
Holehead (Con) said he was not surprised. In his view, few if any of the
Aztecs actually existed.

Councillor Don Binliner (Lab): "Councillor Holehead's attitude is
despicable, racist, fascist and neo-Nazi. The Aztecs, whose ancestors
reached Britain in the seventh century after crossing the Atlantic in stone
boats, represent one of the innumerable waves of immigrants who have
so greatly enriched our society and made it more and more vibrant over
the centuries.

"Together with the millions of Britons, Picts, Romans, Anglo-Saxons,
Danes, Vikings, Flemings, Huguenots and Jews and Irish, leading the
way for some black and Asian immigrants in more recent times, the Aztecs
have helped to make Britain the model multiracial society it is today."

Lost Chords

Is conducting a health hazard, asks my colleague Norman Lebrecht. The
sad death of Giuseppe Sinopoli while conducting *Aida*, and the deaths of
Dmitri Mitropoulos, Eduard van Beinum and other eminent conductors
of the past suggest it may be.

Few conductors can have had more narrow escapes from death, near-
death or apparent death than Sir Jim Gastropodi, formerly conductor of
the Stretchford Municipal Symphony Orchestra. Apparently frail, yet
gifted with dynamic energy, he has fallen off his rickety, rail-less podium
innumerable times, often knocking himself senseless.

At a rehearsal of Mahler's Symphony No 34 ("The Ineradicable") in
1992, he went into such a frenzy in the notorious 40-minute passage for
massed trombones, tubular bells and muted piccoli in the second slow
movement that he fell headlong to the floor, his splintered baton landing
in the open handbag of Miss Tombs, the second harpist.

When a group of his "lads" rushed to help the old man, he sat up and
opened his eyes with a rapt expression and in a low, reverent murmur
told how he had had a "near death" experience. After floating out of his
own body and entering a region of celestial light, he had come face to
face with Mahler.

The composer told him of a hitherto unknown symphony, No 96, known as the "Symphony of a Million" because the entire population of Vienna was to have been forced to take part in its first performance. Sir Jim leant forward reverently as the composer hummed the first bars of the introduction to the fourth slow movement. Then all dissolved in glittering ecstasy as Sir Jim found himself unwillingly gliding back to life with only a fading recollection of a majestic, folkloric, yet overpoweringly ironic theme.

"I shall devote the rest of my life to its recovery," he said, as a look of unearthly rapture transfigured his pallid old face. "At tomorrow's rehearsal we shall begin the search, no?" This did not go down so well with the "lads" as it might have done. Sensing the general mood, Ron Spheroyd, the 22-stone West Riding-born principal bass tuba and Grand High Archmandrite of the Stretchford Basilica of the Musicians' Union (no humble "Father of the Chapel" for him), seized his tuba and blew the stupendous B flat which to musicians everywhere means "All Out!"

Strange Times

Strange times in England, as the all-party anti-racist terror grows in intensity; strange times for the Tory party, when a plain Yorkshireman is condemned and humiliated for trying, however clumsily, to speak the truth, while a smug black lawyer is flattered and cajoled and allowed to lay down the party line.

Race cards of various suits and denominations are twitched from palsied hands and whirled about like withered leaves in a storm of enforced hypocrisy and mixed metaphors. Then the ultimate horror looms. With a bloodcurdling, senile growl, comes the intervention we had dreaded most of all.

Yes, it is Sir Edward Heath in all his monstrous self-celebration. "Look at me," he boasts. "Look how I sacked Enoch Powell when he got out of line! I did not hesitate, oh no! I acted decisively and at once! That is what the present Tory party should have done — what I did."

What is there to boast about in having sacked a truly gifted and patriotic Tory who also tried to tell the truth? Haven't we had enough of Heath's boasting? Away with this very pattern of a self-styled elder statesman! Let him take with him the rewards of a long and — unfortunately for his country — consistent political career. Let him take his testimonials and trophies and pianos and binnacles and unreadable literary works and end his days in a country where he will find himself really appreciated — Communist China.

What the Papers Say

In a thoughtful leader, *The Feudal Times and Reactionary Herald* discusses the recent appointment of "people's peers": "Nothing, we believe, could exceed in crass idiocy, both in conception and execution, this odious, would-be popular measure.

"It is idiotic in theory because, seeming to uphold the natural desire for titles of honour, it defies what alone can justify and dignify such titles: the hereditary principle, the ultimate guarantee of stability in this realm, without which all must collapse in darkness and confusion.

"It is idiotic in execution because this first selection of 'people's peers' has no connection with the 'people' whatever, either in the phantasmal sense of that term which roams the rat-gnawed cerebella of the present government or in the true sense as it has been understood since time immemorial.

"Not surprisingly, the new dignitaries have been greeted with derision by the common people. They are representative of the very class most alien to it. They include fashionable lady scientists, aggressive businessmen and other public figures already supposedly honoured for their part in such pernicious activities as 'public relations', mass education and social control.

"But we believe that the root cause of the common people's derision is not, as commonly stated, their objection to the appointment of such empty figureheads, or their wish to see humble shop assistants, tapsters, or postmen elevated to the peerage instead.

"Rather we believe that the ordinary decent British working man had hoped that the 'people's peers' would be peers in the true sense, in short, that they would comprise the hereditary peers expelled from the House of Lords by the egalitarian malice and modish triviality of foaming radicals and foreign-inspired agitators.

"These are the true people's peers, perceived to be so, we dare aver, by the great body of loyal, patriotic but silenced subjects of the Crown. Until their great voice is heard again, what is this prating about representatives of the people but a bitter mockery?

Cunning

We have to admire the sheer cunning of Tony Blair as he thinks of one vote-catching idea after another in the run-up to the election. First, he has the appealing white calf Phoenix reprieved (votes from animal-lovers: two million?). Then he shows himself subject to ordinary human weakness by publicly assuming new reading glasses (votes from opticians and the short-sighted: 500,000?).

"Bonds for babies" looks like being less successful. But now he has shown his devotion to "law 'n' order", a theme that appeals to natural conservative voters, by staging a spectacular, terrifyingly efficient display of mob control by the police (votes: five million?).

What next? Whatever it is, it will be precisely timed and presented. With the end of the foot and mouth epidemic, a week or so before the election, perhaps, he will announce the Liberation of the Footpaths, with a £10 voucher in compensation for every frustrated rambler and dog-walker and a small packet of biscuits for every dog (votes: six million?).

At intervals, he will offer boons to hospitals, schools, sport and other key beneficiaries. He will arrange a period of glorious summer weather starting a few days before the election (votes: 20 million?).

Will there be a single Tory left in the next Parliament? Or may even the most consummate political cunning sometimes go astray?

An Evil Trade

"Leeds, asylum capital of Britain", declares a *Guardian* article. It tells how 700 immigrant families — Albanian, Bosnian, Somali, Kurdish, Iranian — have settled there in the past year and on the whole are getting on well with the natives.

But there are those who believe that the arrival of these immigrants in the Leeds area is primarily a means of diverting attention from the wholesale smuggling of West Riding people, mainly elderly men, to the Balkans, Iran, Somalia, Kurdistan and the Indian subcontinent. The "grey slave trade," as it is called by the United Nations agencies which are investigating it, has been denounced by militant West Riding dialect societies as "a venomous hundred-headed hydra of our time."

Who were the mysterious 56 elderly Yorkshiremen, wearing flat caps and carrying walking sticks, said by local peasants to speak "with a marked accent, with diphthong peculiarities and labio-fricatives commonly associated with the Pudsey district", who were seen landing from a dinghy near Karachi and hurriedly making their way inland one moonlit night in March?

Why did a fully equipped, prefabricated British Legion hut, with the emblem of a well-known Yorkshire brewery hanging outside appear overnight in a suburb of Peshawar?

Although Pakistan seems to be a favourite destination, a great number of these pathetic deluded immigrants make for Albania and Kosovo in their search for a better life. Yet the fragments of traditional Yorkshire wisdom they continually proffer in their incredibly slow speech — "They should never have started it." "What you want is a thorough good shaking" — must have helped to drive many Albanians even further out of their minds than they were to start with.

Who are the sinister exploiters behind this infamous traffic in credulous humanity? Immigrants from Leeds to places like Karachi, Isfahan, Pristina, Qom and Mogadishu, find they are by no means as welcome there as immigrants from these places seem to be in Leeds. Some, robbed of their flat caps and walking sticks by giant Pathan moneylenders, are subject to gross humiliations. They may be forced to act as substitutes for dancing bears freed by animal rights workers.

The "big boys" in this hideous trade are believed to operate from places like Ilkley, Trieste, Zonguldak and Pateley Bridge.

They also use the island of Socotra in the Arabian Sea, as an entrepot for despatch of the Yorkshiremen to Pakistan, either in rusting old cargo or pilgrimage vessels or, like a well-known illegal immigrant of former days, Sinbad the Sailor, on the back of a giant roc.

C.H. Hunzvi

Mrs M. Dutt-Pauker writes: "Many of us who eagerly followed the people's struggle against white colonialism in the former Rhodesia will think with affection of Dr Chenjerai 'Hitler' Hunzvi, the distinguished leader of the Zimbabwean war veterans' movement, who died this week.

"As a young freedom fighter in exile from his native land, Chenjerai often stayed with us at Marxmount or at my other homes, Glynstalin, Leninmore Castle and Craig Gramscie, in the intervals of his Marxist medical studies in Eastern Europe.

"Always excellent company, he was a great favourite with the children, particularly my daughter Deirdre, who was entranced by his tales of daring exploits against the white racists. These were to culminate later on in his campaign — not yet concluded — to rid Zimbabwe of every vestige of its former oppressors.

"His claim that he 'hated all white people' was taken by all of us in good part, as a typically colourful expression of his firmly progressive, anti-racist stance. He had a keen sense of humour, and, I believe, playfully adopted the somewhat unconventional nickname 'Hitler' in order to tease the white Rhodesian fascists, most of whom, of course, had sympathised strongly with their fellow German fascists during the war.

"He will be greatly missed, not only by his many friends but by all who support the cause of anti-racism, whether in Zimbabwe or here at home."

Resistance

Donating £5 million to the Conservative Party, Sir Paul Getty says he believes it is "the party best-equipped to defend the British way of life". When Labour came to power in 1997, this wise and percipient American said: "It's probably true that the Britain I love is not the Britain which exists today. But it is still closer to that than anything else. And I think that the attempt by politicians to create a new image for Britain will be resisted."

In the past four years resistance has gradually dwindled, and the Britain worth loving is now further away than ever. If only out of gratitude, Conservative politicians, as they accept Sir Paul's money, should try to embody that resistance. At present, they are assailed from every side with advice to "move to the middle ground"; "drop all Right-wing (that is, Conservative) tendencies"; "accept the tolerant, inclusive Britain of today", and so on and so forth.

That is the very last thing they should do. The "middle ground" is where almost everything that is wrong with this country flourishes and proliferates. It is the home of Left-liberal orthodoxy, of every kind of fashionable nonsense, of moral degeneracy, "political correctness" and "anti-racism", trash culture, vulgar barbarism, submission to the mob as well as militant homosexuality and feminism, mindless worship of "change" and, above all, the false and pernicious doctrine of human equality.

A true Conservative programme would repudiate all that. Here are a few "guidelines" which Central Office will have to work out in detail and present to the public in a more attractive form.

Home affairs: withdraw all subsidies to the Commission for Racial

Equality, the Equal Opportunities Commission and all other anti-discriminatory rackets; repudiate the Macpherson Report and re-establish the traditional British police force.

Constitutional Reform: refashion devolution and restore the United Kingdom of Great Britain and Ireland; restore the hereditary House of Lords, with greater powers than before.

Education: reduce the school leaving age to 12, leading to the abolition of compulsory education altogether.

Health: abolition of all public health services. Electoral reform: restrict the franchise by applying educational and property qualifications; abolish votes for women.

Defence: a big programme of expansion for the armed forces, particularly the Navy. Foreign policy: denounce all "European" treaties and agreements; work for Anglo-Russian alliance.

As for the present contenders for the leadership of the party — Portillo, Clarke, Duncan Smith, Widdecombe, "Madonna", Gypsy Petulengro, Horatio Bottomley — who among these could be trusted to present these policies to a nation dying for want of them? Discuss.

In Deep Space

American astronomers have discovered an "icy object large enough to qualify as a planet" orbiting the sun between Neptune and Pluto. "When we spotted it, we just wrote 'wow' on the image. We knew right away it was a big one." An objectionable thing about these astronomers is their complete lack of respect for celestial phenomena, invariably expressed in vulgar, facetious language.

Our own discoveries, relayed from the columnar space vehicle "Don Carlos and the Holy Alliance III", now motoring in deep space, have quite a different tone. The findings are also different. Instead of miscellaneous lumpish icy objects, they have found, in the vast spaces between Neptune and Pluto, a number of delightful little worlds, beautifully varied with hill and dale, woodland, lakes, trout streams and broad uplands abounding in game of every kind.

Many of the great feudal landowners of Pluto, it seems, are also proprietors of these little private worlds, where they hunt, shoot and fish to their hearts' content. They have enviable hunting lodges, well equipped with billiard rooms and libraries. On their shelves are leather-bound volumes of the *Plutonian Field* and *Plutonian Country Life*; also (though this awaits arrival and analysis of the daguerreotypes), complete runs of the *Racing Calendar* and first editions of *Surtees*.

An Awkward Guest

The "international community" seeks to arrest Dr Radovan Karadzic, the Bosnian Serb leader, as a "war criminal" and try him before the bogus international court at the Hague. Should we offer him asylum in this column?

With his picturesque appearance, his poetical gifts, his degree in psychology, his skill at playing on the guzle, his witty conversation, his romantic personality and charm, Dr Karadzic has always been something of a favourite here. But how would he "fit in"? Would he miss terribly the life of intrigue, violence and danger he has been used to?

We might grant him a small estate in our eastern mountains or on the western seaboard looking on the Dreaded Void. Or he might find congenial employment as a bard and story-teller in the castle of some great nobleman, enchanting high and low with fantastic tales of his native land.

But he would have to be discouraged from the outset from taking part in military activities, however tempted he might be to form the nomadic tribesmen of our northern frontier into a formidable guerrilla force, linking it with "adventurist elements" and their "hare-brained plans" to cross the Interpaginal Channel and seize the north-eastern regions of the opposite page, according to tradition the columnar motherland.

Should Dr Karadzic's restless energies become a threat to the paginal balance of power, leading to a crisis whose outcome no man could foresee, then he would have to go. It would be painful for us to send him back to the terrible world outside, the world of "human rights" lawyers, of humbugging liberal verbalisers armed with advanced weaponry, the world of Albright and Cook and Clinton and other such monsters of the "international community". But at least he has had plenty of experience of coping with them.

In the Bunker

With the mounting threat to all he holds dear, J. Bonington Jagworth, Britain's most eminent motorist, called a plenary session of his Motorists' Liberation front in its luxurious inspection-pit headquarters "somewhere near Staines".

Sloshing a quadruple "BGA" into his silver presentation hub-cap and adding a dash of his favourite brake-fluid, the leader addressed his paladins in a voice like the revving of a dozen racing cars. "Serious motoring is under attack as never before. The levy on motorists entering central London, the shameful surrender of the Hastings by-pass, the sneaky police speed-trap/cameras now appearing all over the bloody place. But what use are words? We must act.

"How about blockading the motorways? What do you say to a force of a hundred Boggs/Superoafs driving into London — I would lead it, of course — and forcing its way into Parliament itself? Put the fear of God into those wretched ecofreaks and pedestrian-collaborators! Can't you just see those miserable creeps who've never done a crafty 150 on a motorway in their lives — can't you just see the sheer terror on their pasty faces?"

The Rev John Goodwheel, chaplain-general to the MLF, known to millions as the "Apostle of the motorways", had been shifting uneasily in his place and nervously touching the gold pectoral spanner that hangs from his fur-lined clerical collar with oil-stained yet pious fingers.

"With the greatest respect, JB," he murmured, "I cannot wholeheartedly support this. While understandable, it will merely alienate the general public. The days when we serious motorists dreamt of taking over the whole world are gone. We are now a dwindling breed. Yet as our strength lessens, stronger grows our courage."

"True, but it may well be that in a generation we motorists will be no more than a persecuted sect, condemned to practise our rites of worship in the modern equivalent of the catacombs in a very real sense."

Jagworth glared, speechless with anger. "Keep your religion out of it," sneered Royston Cylinder, the crypto-Marxist chief-of-staff. "We must believe in the future. What did Gramsci say? "Pessimism of the intellect; optimism of the will.""

"Who's this Gramsci chap? Jagworth asked. "An Eyetie by the sound of him. Say what you like about the Eyeties, they do know something about real motoring. What sort of car did he drive anyhow? A Maserati? Ferrari? Or the original 30-cylinder Ombra Mai-fu? Ah, that was a real car for you!" For a moment he was lost in memories of desperate Alpine corniches taken at 90 on two wheels, of roaring garages full of the heroes of old.

"Gramsci," droned Cylinder, "was a great opponent of Mussolini who spent a lot of time in prison." "Then what on earth is the point of him?" Jagworth roared. "Now, gentlemen, to business . . ."

Among the Bones

The search for the earliest hominid which, according to accepted theories diverged from the chimpanzee to become the earliest human being, is growing ever more complicated, even frantic. Last year, a team of French palaeontologists, working in Kenya, announced their discovery of "Millennium Man", a creature pieced together from 13 fossilised bones, provisionally dated as living six million years ago. A rival American team, working in Ethiopia, has now deduced from a collection of bones, including a jawbone with teeth, a hominid dated at between 5.8 and 5.2 million years ago.

Dr John Goodbone, head of the palaeontology department at Nerdley University, is not one to take this lying down. At a recent dig at his favourite site near the Star of Bangladesh Takeaway Curry Institute on the old Nerdley bypass, he unearthed a collection of bones of all sizes and quickly assembled them into a hominid he calls Homo Eoparanthropopithecus Nerdleiensis, dated at seven million years ago.

This hominid, he believes, could walk upright or on all fours or on its elbows and heels, and could probably do all these things at the same time, frightening predators to death. It had at least three sets of teeth, one with amalgam fillings which, Dr Goodbone thinks, may force us to revise our views of the state of dentistry seven million years ago. The extra teeth would have been useful at the time of the extinction of the dinosaurs and the growth of giant truffles and Brussels sprouts.

"But we know all too little of the conditions he will have faced at that time. Certainly a modern person transported back to that era would most probably have noticed the absence of many things we take for granted, such as pop groups, call centres and betting shops. But, like all the other certified hominids discovered so far, it comes from Africa and is free of racist tendencies. Not that it had to come far. Owing to the shifting of the tectonic plates, Nerdley, six million years ago, was part of Africa anyhow."

Books and Reading

Saddam Hussein's new novel *Zabibah and the King* is top of the charts in Baghdad, with rave reviews in the state-controlled press. It is also much talked about in Stretchford, where the typical housewives' Our Saddam Hussein Fan Club has managed to obtain a copy.

"It's an absolutely enthralling read. I literally could not put this book down," says Mrs Linda Gumbs, 49, the club secretary. "But I do wish it wasn't printed in this peculiar backwards writing. I have written to Saddam, asking for an English translation, but no reply so far. The Americans must have intercepted it with their golf-ball domes."

Mrs Gumbs has put an advertisement in the *Stretchford Clarion's* book page: "A staggering new genius has risen like an asteroid over the horizon of world literature. Mr Hussein has a rare ability to probe the recesses of the human heart and drag out raw, palpitating lumps of insight. Everybody should read this book, or else."

As though by an ineluctable law, the rival Anti-Our Saddam Hussein Fan Club has put an announcement on the same page: "It is a remarkable comment on contemporary values that Mr Hussein can take time off from devising vital weapons of mass destruction to write this pathetic, sentimental drivel. It makes Edna O'Brien seem like Dante Alegretto (*sic*)."

Detachments of the rival groups, armed with sawn-off stubby umbrellas and outsize lead-weighted handbags, clashed outside the Hanging Gardens of Babylon Hyperconsumerama in Victoria Square. After a personal appeal from Supt J.S. Harrogate, 52, the police fan club squad supremo and secretary of the local Pre-Raphaelite Circle, both sides withdrew, then joined in traditional looting, described as "moderate to severe", of the organic cat food section of the Hyperconsumerama, in which section commander Ken Tombs, 37, sustained injuries to the ballpoint pen.

"I have been here before, but when or how I cannot tell," Supt Harrogate commented later, while Blackie, eight, the squad cat, stared at him with baleful yellow eyes through dried sunflowers in a tall, hastily supplied magenta vase.

Patriot

For General Sir Walter Walker, who has died at 88, I had a warmer regard than for almost any British general of the last century. In appearance and manner he was everything a British general should be. A superb commander, he was distinguished for brilliant campaigns that put paid to communist insurgents in Malaya and Borneo.

He was also distinguished for having the right opinions and never hesitated to express them. He deplored the shameful surrender of Rhodesia to communist savagery. He favoured strong measures against the IRA. He thought Enoch Powell would make a good prime minister. He warned us tirelessly against communist enemies both at home and abroad.

With all this, he made plenty of enemies himself.

In the Seventies, he set up an organisation called "Civil Association", a force of volunteers which would be ready to take over essential services if, as then seemed possible, public order should break down. It soon had 100,000 supporters. Such an organisation, patriotic and conservative in the true sense, was bound to attract the sneering ridicule of every Hampstead thinker and smug Left-liberal verbaliser in the country, and this it did in full measure.

When it petered out, one more chance of rousing the country from its habitual torpor was lost. Gen Walker had spoken in a newspaper interview of the Army having to take over the government. But he was far too much of a gentleman, I think, and far too nice a man to make a military dictator.

Thirty years later, a nation no longer threatened with foreign conquest or internal revolution, but sunk in witless hedonism and commercial barbarism, seems helpless before the creeping advance of a different kind of dictatorship — the dictatorship of the Blairite one-party state. Instead of patriotism and care for its own people, it favours multi-racialism at home and "progressive" war abroad on behalf of a bogus and sinister "international community".

Who will stand against it? Walter Walker was a fine example of a certain type of Englishman. Is that type altogether extinct?

Safety first

Sir Aylwin Goth-Jones, the genial, unpopular chief constable of Stretchford, is a keen speed camera fan. He has ordered a thousand new ones to be installed all over the conurbation. They will be painted in purple, scarlet, emerald green and his own favourite, "butcher blue". Amanda Goth-Jones, his niece, artist-in-residence at Nerdley central police station, has produced some arresting designs based on paintings by Picasso, Dali, Tracey Emin, Bouguereau and other great masters.

At a hastily summoned press conference, Sir Aylwin answered critics who thought that the new cameras, far from preventing accidents, would fascinate drivers to the point of losing control. The point of the new cameras, he said, was to build bridges between motorists, the police, artists and the public. The arts had long been deprived of their proper role in dealing with problems of road safety. Here was a chance to fill a gap in the cultural life of the nation, which, if unfilled, might make a philistine Britain the laughing stock of the civilised world.

Asked if it was true that police officers monitoring the cameras were betting on the registration numbers of speeding motorists, sometimes for large sums, Sir Aylwin said that officers engaged in this somewhat monotonous work needed to enliven it with a "bit of fun".

"I sometimes drop in myself to take a hand. The other day I made a real killing with a 50-1 bet on an 'H and double three' combination. I had to stand brandy and cigars from the canteen all round."

Scramble!

When Mrs Eileen Briggs, 57, reported the theft of a favourite watering can from her garden in Kandahar Road, Lampton-on-Hove, three police helicopters were immediately scrambled and circled the neighbourhood for 40 minutes.

When the crew, with other armed officers and a full complement of dog-handlers, paramedics, forensic experts, social workers, stress counsellors and Kurdish interpreters, located Mrs Briggs, she stated that the watering can was not the one she had supposed and was not missing anyhow. Neighbours complained that the continual buzzing of helicopters "made them feel stressed". Some said it "was like living in Macedonian-occupied Palestine or something".

"A routine storm in a teacup," stated Sir Aylwin Goth-Jones, 55, the genial, unpopular Chief Constable of Stretchford. "I'm a firm believer in the use of helicopters for police work and only wish I had a hundred at my disposal. My officers love flying about in them, so they're good for morale. They come to me saying: 'Sir, please sir, what about us having some real helicopter gunships, like, with machine-guns and rockets? Oh, why can't we, please, sir?' It breaks my heart to have to refuse them. It's a real policing problem for our day and age in a very real sense," he added in a strangely altered, declamatory tone.

Some of the young officers' romantic dreams are fired by conversations they have, off duty in the Quantity Surveyors' Arms off the old Nerdley by-pass with the self-promoted RAF veteran and self-styled Battle of Britain pilot, Group Captain "Jumbo" Goth-Jones, black sheep of his family. He is the sole survivor of Stretchford City Council's planning department's air reconnaissance squadron, once the terror of "dodgy" building developers, pig-keepers defying the environmental health regulations, unlicensed caravan-site promoters and, in the private sector, faithless housewives and their milkmen lovers and other potential subjects for blackmail.

Swashbuckling, handlebar-moustached, blazered, purple-nosed "Jumbo" fascinates the young policemen over pints of Directors' bitter, watched by a sardonic, yawning barman, with tales of his bygone exploits in the Stretchford skies. He will tell, over and over again, how, "zooming along at nought feet" over Nerdley, his "old kite" was riddled by the crack potato-machine-gun marksmen of Bog Lane Secondary Modern School. "Mind you, I could have pressed the red tit and ejected! But I battled on regardless and brought her down, with light ale streaming from her port engine, in just about the hairiest landing of my flying career," he drones on like his own aircraft. The wide-eyed policemen listen, transported to a magic realm of comradeship and adventure, more determined than ever to fly, one day, the mighty helicopter of their desire.

A Hero of Our Time

One of the few "ethnic minorities" not represented at the great UN Conference against Racism, Racial Discrimination, Xenophobia and Related Intolerance is the Aztec community of Nerdley. Its absence is due to what Royston Huizilopoctli (formerly Royston Nobes), its South Shields-born 42nd-year sociology student leader, has denounced as a deliberate insult.

"As leader of an important ethnic minority, an eminent sociologist and probably the greatest authority on anti-racism in Britain, I naturally expected an invitation to join the British delegation in an advisory capacity.

"I have been pointedly ignored. This slight will never be forgotten or forgiven, either by me or by my people. You know me. When thwarted, I am implacable. Henceforth it is war to the knife — to the obsidian knife! Mass human sacrifice! Thousands of hearts shall bleed!"

At a hastily summoned joint press conference with Cllr Don Binliner, chairman of the Nerdley Borough Council Anti-racist Outreach Committee, he made the Aztec position clear. "We demand an apology from the Spanish government for the atrocities committed by the racist, fascist Conquistadors who invaded our country, slaughtered and enslaved our people and destroyed our ancient civilisation.

"We also demand financial compensation of an amount to be agreed, plus 500 years' compound interest, to be divided equally between ourselves and our compatriots in Mexico."

A foolish journalist pointed out that according to the Aztec community's own historians, their ancestors left what is now Mexico 700 years before the Spanish invasion, crossing the Atlantic in stone boats, pushing inland by way of what is now the Manchester Ship Canal and founding settlements in and around what is now the Nerdley central public reference library in Carbon Brush Street.

"A typical racist attitude," Huitzilopochtli roared. "It is high time you white people understood the sorrow and triumph of our Aztec diaspora, which gives us all the more right to speak for the whole of our race. To this day, in the so-called Stretchford Conurbation, we have been victims of continual racism, racial discrimination, xenophobia and related intolerance of every kind you can think of.

"A particularly evil bit of related intolerance is the slander put about by racists, fascists, Tory extremists and Right-wing lunatics that our Aztec community does not exist, but is merely a collection of drop-outs, welfare scroungers, illegal immigrants, squatters and New Age travellers. We demand another apology for this slur, plus extra compensation. We also demand the abolition of the monarchy, gay and lesbian subsidies and British troops out of Ireland."

Deirdre's Way

Life at Marxmount, Mrs Dutt-Pauker's fine white mansion on the edge of Hampstead Heath, has been troubled lately by noisy altercations and occasional explosions, audible even through the green baize door of the nursery wing. They are part of the ongoing ideological struggle between Bert Brecht Mao Che Odinga, Deirdre's bearded little activist son, and Gjoq, the Albanian au pair girl.

"Of course, I simply adore the Albanians," Deirdre often says. But her offers to join the National Liberation Army in Kosovo were repeatedly rebuffed, and lately she has begun to sympathise with Bert's revisionist, pro-Milosevic stand against the "unreconstructed" Maoist Gjoq, who has denounced the NLA as "a pathetic bunch of middle-class fluffies".

Wandering the cedared lawns of Marxmount, disconsolate for want of a good liberal cause, Deirdre found one instantly when she heard of the Australian government's unhelpful attitude towards Afghan refugees and, even more horrifying, the Australian people's enthusiastic support for it. One moment pale and listless, the next she was mechanically shouting, "Boycott Australian goods!"

It was like being back in the glorious days of old, when she had blundered through many a supermarket, boldly snatching South African grapefruit from the trolleys of bewildered old ladies and cans of Fosters from bewildered old men, who promptly snatched them back again. It was even more like the old days when, seeking the Australian High Commission to shout a few slogans outside it, she found herself, by force of habit, outside the old South African embassy across the way, shouting "Release Mandela — Now!"

She might have been arrested if a group of social workers had not hustled her away for a counselling session with a view to talking through her evident personality difficulties. When she got back to Marxmount, she found her mother arguing with a police inspector who was being far too slow in ejecting some Afghan "asylum seekers" from her immaculate domains.

No Change

Only a stony-hearted fanatic could have been unmoved by the massacre in America. Yet for us feudal landlords and clerical reactionaries, cranks, conspiracy theorists and luddite peasants, the downfall of the twin towers that symbolised the worldwide empire of imaginary money is not in itself a cause of grief.

Ever since the atrocity, dense clouds of hysterical rhetoric have been drifting about the world. America is at war, says President Bush. Britain is at war, says Tony Blair, dutifully echoing his master. The whole world is at war, say the "media". But what enemy is the world at war against? Terrorism!

A war against terrorism is as futile and fatuous as those other fashionable wars, "the war against drugs" and "the war against racism". You might as well declare war against old age or death.

September 11, the "media" say, was the day that changed the world for ever. But the world has not changed. It is still the same old world, good and bad, that it has always been. As for terrorism and terror, only one thing is certain: we have seen nothing yet.

Provincial News

In Stretchford, the hunt for Osama bin Laden is on. He has been seen in every part of the conurbation, sometimes in several places at once. A tall, brooding figure, unmistakable for his deep-set, prune-like eyes and evil beard, he has been seen walking alone in lovely, sex maniac-haunted Sadcake Park. He has been glimpsed in the seldom visited galleries of the National Museum of Rubber Bands; on the Arthur Grudge Memorial Nature Trail; and even in the spacious aisles of the tinned catfood section of the Nadirco Hyperconsumerama.

The hunt is on for all the Afghan terrorists, believed to be lurking everywhere, who, at any rate temporarily, have replaced farmers as objects of hate and suspicion. The city council department of information has issued a leaflet, "Afghan Terrorists: how to spot them", illustrated with artists' impressions:

"Your average Afghan terrorist will be bearded, wearing a loose robe and 'towel-type' headdress or hard hat plainly marked 'Jihad (or holy war)', part of his disguise as a building worker. He will be carrying a home-made rifle or machine-gun, and will be draped with one or more ammunition belts. Do not 'have a go' or try to tempt him with cigarettes or alcohol (he will reject both), but report your sighting (on the form supplied) to the nearest social service centre, where qualified experts will be available to deal with him."

One of the most serious dangers is the formation of a typical housewives' Our Oscar van Leyden (*sic*) fan club, followed, as by an ineluctable law, by its Anti-Our Oswald van Linden (*sic*) corollary. At a rumour that detachments of both rival factions were marching on the city centre, a cry of "racism" went up.

Immediately students of Stretchford University were alerted by their representative council for a mass demonstration. At least they should have been. But it was not like the old days. Slowly a few dozen students roused themselves from staring at electronic games in cannabis-suffused bed-sitters, or in beer-drenched canteens, broke off their discussions on the number of female students they had respectively seduced. Some vaguely recalling the drill movements of old times, reached feebly for dusty, moth-eaten banners ("Second Front Now!" "Arms for Spain!" "Yanks out of Nicaragua!").

In the city centre, a single tall housewife arose like a prophetess of old to bar their way. A thin rain began to fall. From the distance came a mysterious brazen uproar. Whimpering with fear of the unknown, the pathetic shades of a once mighty army of the Left drifted away.

Rebuked

My use of the term "Blairite Junta" has drawn a dignified rebuke from the secretary-general of the World Association of Military Juntas, whose headquarters are in the Central American Republic of Costaguana: "My association considers the term 'junta' wholly inapplicable to Mr Blair and his ministers and an unacceptable slight on our members.

"Juntas, alas, are now an endangered species, and misuse of the term does not help their survival. Mr Blair may perhaps claim to be leader of a coterie or clique. But a true junta consists of a group of swarthy, moustached military officers of Hispanic appearance, wearing dark glasses and slightly soiled white tropical uniforms with plenty of gold braid and medal-ribbons. They meet in a room with fans in the ceiling and a view of palm trees through the window, and are usually occupied in signing death-warrants.

"As far as my information goes, Mr Blair and his associates have none of these essential attributes. An apology and a substantial sum of Third World Aid, to be agreed, would go some way to redressing your no doubt unintended slight on my association."

Bridge Building

In a bold move in the "war against terrorism", Dr Spacely-Trellis, the go-ahead Bishop of Stretchford, is organising a series of workshops in his cathedral. "What is absolutely essential", he told a group of senior "anti-racist" and trans-faith executives gathered in the People's Narthex, "is to get a relevant, meaningful dialogue going between the Taliban and the West in a spirit of mutual understanding and, above all, compassion;  to build an enduring bridge between us in a very real sense.

"I am bringing together a panel of distinguished experts representing all shades of opinion. To name a few: Dr Wendy Dutt-Pauker, head of the department of anti-police studies at Stretchford University; Dr Heinz Kiosk, the eminent social psychologist; his colleague and partner, Dr Melisande Fischbein; and Dr Neville Dreadberg, the distinguished novelist, sculptor, playwright, composer, TV producer and multimedia Renaissance Man.

"Then we have Dr Tamsin Alibi-Jones, director of the Race Relations Industrial Council; Dr Greg Blowhard, head of demonstrational studies at Gnomesall Heath University; Dr Abdul Castrumba, the great neo-Koranic scholar and emeritus professor of social subversion at Soup Hales University; and many more.

"Truly a galaxy of intellect. I had hoped to include Dr Osama bin Laden, the distinguished Islamic expert, to add his very distinctive voice to our deliberations, but, alas, he is not available at the moment. However, I am hoping to get one or two representatives of the Taliban. The keynote of our workshops will be, above all, a broad-based ecumenism.

"I am convinced that the Taliban does not consist only, or even mainly, of the religious extremists we are told about by our ill-informed media. It must include many rational, well-disposed, caring people like ourselves. I know they are keen to learn all about the issues that are so important to us: human rights, gay and lesbian rights — I believe that they are just as angry about the scandal of Section 28, for example, as we are — and sex education as well as decent health services, of course, and public transport.

"I am convinced they are ready to give up their primitive, outmoded superstitions about Allah, the Prophet and so on, just as we have given up our primitive, outmoded superstitions about God, the Trinity, the saints and all the rest. They are anxious to find a secular faith suited to our day and age, a faith that meets the needs of the average man and woman of today, whether in Kabul or London. In short, they are anxious to join the modern world in a very real sense."

As the audience applauded, he put on his mitre, adding, to the wonder of all, an "Arafat-type" head-dress on top, then prostrated himself on an ecumenical prayer rug specially woven for the occasion by Ethnicaids Textiles. The Rev Mantissa Shout, rural dean of Nerdley and the bishop's partner, smiled invisibly beneath her elegant, "Taliban-type" silk burka, while Dr Rashid Iftikarullah, the Grand Mufti of Stretchford, who had brought his 25 children along with him, added a thunderous, ecumenical-type guffaw to their merry, tinkling laughter.

Heart of the Matter

In his efforts to enlist Arab countries for his coalition, President Bush is said to have supported the idea of a Palestinian state, "so long as the right of Israel to exist is respected". But after all that has happened, would the people of any conceivable Palestinian state regard this as a right at all? For the Israelis, to accept such a plan might mean suicide; to reject it might mean that America would desert them. What a dilemma!

From their own point of view, would the Israelis have done better, at the height of their military success in 1967, to occupy the whole of what we used to call the Holy Land, expelling the Arab inhabitants if need be?

If this sounds like a bit of old-fashioned machtpolitik, there are precedents for it, not only in the Old Testament, but in more recent times. At the end of the Second World War, millions of Germans were expelled, for the benefit of Poles and Czechs, from lands where they had lived for centuries. Nobody except the victims objected. Could the Israelis have got away with it?

That is a matter for conjecture. But it is not necessary to believe in ancient prophecies to feel, with deep foreboding, that the key to everything that is happening in the Middle East, indeed, to everything that is happening in the world, is in the Holy Land.

What the Papers Say

In a thoughtful leader, The *Feudal Times and Reactionary Herald* offers an alternative prospect for the world to that of Tony Blair: "Now that our rebellious North American colonists, justifiably enraged by the late atrocities in their country, have put themselves on a war footing, few will doubt that we have a certain family duty to help these wayward but redoubtable people in their time of trouble.

"Few will doubt, however, that the price of our support must be their concurrence with a general settlement in the world: a return to the principles of sanity that were so disastrously overturned by their own revolt and by the even more lamentable events that followed it in France.

"First and foremost, we must assert the superiority of our own European civilisation — a principle left to an Italian politician (whose name escapes us) to enunciate some time ago, to the scorn and derision, needless to say, of the enemies of our civilisation in our own country and abroad.

"We must restore the stability and good government formerly assured by colonial rule in Africa, Asia and South America. A reunited India must again accept the benevolent authority of the Raj. The Chinese Empire, too, must be restored together with its admirable mandarinate.

"In Europe itself, the empires and monarchies which were so lamentably swept away after the First World War, must rise again, ensuring those civilities of diplomacy temporarily replaced by a graceless rabble of ignorant upstarts, low-bred bagmen and radical students. But the price of our support for our rebel colonists in their present trouble must be an end to their present anomalous position which, thanks in part to our own supine policies, has now lasted for more than 200 years.

"We are convinced that the better sort among our rebel colonists would welcome a new declaration of allegiance to Crown and Empire. Sentiment apart, who can doubt that the Empire, newly invigorated by the return of these impetuous but energetic people, would be the dominant power in the world for the foreseeable future, unchallenged by any power or combination of powers that could be brought against it?"

Progress

I have never been in Afghanistan. But with a bit more enterprise I might have got there. One day towards the end of the Second World War, it was my duty to conduct a party of Afghan army officers round military installations in Bengal. They were affable and courteous men, whose legendary ferocity, if it existed at all, was well under control.

They spoke little English and not much Urdu. But one general, who had studied at the Potsdam Military Academy in the old days, spoke good German. He spoke of the beauties of his native land, of Persian poetry and of his own rose gardens in Kabul. "When the war is over, I hope you will come and see them for yourself."

I shall never see the rose gardens of Kabul now; nor, I dare say, will anybody else. That charming Afghan must long ago have perished with them, as the filthy tides of communism and progress, made more devastating still by the ferocity of warring tribesmen, surged to and fro over everything that was civilised in Afghanistan, obliterating its gardens and all its other treasures, and leaving nothing but a brave and noble people struggling to live among the ruins.

Fifty years later, here comes another tide of destruction in the name of progress, freedom, democracy and the international community.

Calling All Bores

A bright new star has risen over the all too nebulous horizon of British boring! Are aficionados of the yawn game (writes "Narcolept") going to have something to cheer about at last?

Who is this new home-grown master of lethargy? Not only is he a bore of formidable talent; he is black to boot.

It is a sad reflection on our multiracial society that our black community has so far had little impact on top-class boring. There are boring fans, I'm ashamed to say, who maintain that there is an inherent lack of yawn-making ability among black people, and that it is this, rather than deliberate discrimination, that has kept black men and women out. I believe, on the contrary, that your average black man and woman has everything it takes to reach the pinnacles of the yawnster's art.

So step forward, "Lord" Taylor, new black hope of multiracial British boredom! This gifted "life peer" was scarcely known until he astounded the world by failing to get elected as a Conservative in a by-election at Cheltenham. Since then he has been working away at the boring theme he has made his own, a theme of infinite promise: the failure of the Conservative Party to devote all its time to extirpating racism among its members.

Yes, it's a winner all right. In my view, and I speak with some authority, I think, it is a theme to rank with oil-fired central heating, parking problems in Ongar, or the history of the League of Nations Union as a cast-iron, copper-bottomed, eyelid drooping, jaw-dislocating knock-out.

Go to it, "Lord" Taylor! Keep this theme of supreme boredom rolling, and one day, I believe, we shall see you up there among the great greats, boring for Britain with such titans of the intergalactic yawn game as Jean-Pierre Cafard of Canada, R.S. Nattcharya of India and Shloime ben Chloroform ("Glorious Shloime"), Israel's superhuman bore of bores!

Correction

Not long ago, I mistakenly referred to Mantissa Shout, Dr Spacely-Trellis's partner, as the "Rural Dean of Stretchford". She is, of course, the Countryside Dean. According to Dr Trellis himself, this is "reflecting the new, progressive role of the British countryside in a very real sense".

Mantissa herself has the wellbeing of the countryside very much at heart. She is a keen supporter of the Stretchford branch of the Hunt Saboteurs' Association. She is prominent in the militant ramblers' movement and took part in a recent mass-trespass on the estate of Lord Haversnake, in which the aged peer, crippled from a war wound, was tipped out of his wheelchair and made to carry a placard reading, "I am a Neo-Nazi".

Mantissa is often seen at anti-farming demonstrations, wearing the elegant silk hijab that denotes her sympathy with the Muslim community. She carries Mr Prescott's injunction to be "nice to Muslims" to what some think extreme lengths. She can never see a Muslim in the street without going up to him or her with a cheerful "Salaam Aleikum. Good morning. I am Mantissa Shout, the Bishop's partner. How are you doing these days? I hope you are coping with the problem of white racism?", followed by a terrifyingly jolly laugh and a promise of a home visit soon.

Not all Muslims appreciate this. Some have asked Dr J.S. Iftikarullah, the Grand Mufti of Stretchford, if he can see his way to issuing a small fatwa against her. But so far, mindful of his inter-faith solidarity with the Bishop, the wily cleric has refrained.

Watch this Space

Demonstrators in London last week carried placards, one reading "We are not at War; Stop the War", the other, "Stop the Racist Backlash; Defend Civil Liberties". The second pair of slogans, though less obviously absurd, are no less self-contradictory.

One of the latest threats to civil liberties is a proposed supplement to the infamous laws against "racism" which would make "incitement to religious hatred" a criminal offence punishable by up to seven years in jail. In principle, any discussion about any religion, even in private, could become a "hate crime".

This is one of a whole class of newly invented "crimes". All of them are designed ostensibly to protect minorities from the majority. But in practice they all serve to increase the power of the state over all its subjects. When next Tony Blair delivers one of his gaseous orations about freedom and democracy, remember this.

Tidings of Joy

By *Mungo Clange*

Did you see that lovely photograph in Tuesday's paper, I mean the one that showed Tony Blair shaking hands with Yasser Arafat in Downing Street? And did it, I wonder, bring you the same warm feeling of oneness that I had?

Both leaders had lovely smiles that owed something — but not everything, of course — to the skill of British and Palestinian dentists respectively. But as they gazed with such obvious sincerity into each other's eyes, I thought Yasser's smile was just that little bit more sincere than Tony's.

Yasser's smart brown uniform, with a row of pens — or could they be bullets? — clipped to the breast pocket, contrasted beautifully with Tony's well-cut, grey civilian suit and sober blue tie. As the meeting was indoors, Tony followed our British custom by remaining hatless.

But I couldn't help thinking how much more impressive the symbolism of British-Muslim friendship might have been if Tony, rather than Yasser, had been wearing that delightful chequered head-dress — keffiyeh, I believe it's called — with the long tassel hanging down like a bell-pull, just asking for someone to give it a playful tug!

There's nothing like an exchange of headgear, I always think, for building bridges between the different communities of our multicultural Britain. Only the other day the Prince of Wales himself was photographed wearing a traditional Muslim cap and shawl when he visited a London mosque. And one of our best-loved politicians, Lord Hattersley, has been seen wearing all kinds of ethnic headgear — turbans, Gandhi caps, skull caps and once, if I'm not mistaken, a yashmak.

I do hope the idea catches on. If all the Muslims in Bradford, for instance, started wearing our traditional top hats and straw boaters instead of turbans and fezzes, what wonders it might do for inter-community relations. And the same goes for those obstinate folk in Northern Ireland. I'd love to see Gerry Adams wearing a bowler hat and orange sash and all the trimmings, wouldn't you?

I do hope you agree with me. And will you write to me about it? I'm sure you will.

Armchair War

Whatever the merits of the "war against terrorism", if any, it is a poor sort of war for us armchair warriors, red-faced blimps, retired colonels and the like. In the old days, wars had definite battle fronts, pincer movements, advances and retreats. What could be more pleasant than to settle down in one's study, where the maps are spread on table and wall, with some good claret to drink, a good log fire burning and, if possible, rain lashing the windows?

One has read the latest reports from the battle-fronts in one's well-ironed newspapers at breakfast. Now one can bring out the talc and Chinagraph pencils and little flags with pins, and get busy with the maps. It is the image of war without its guilt and with none of its danger whatsoever.

One could spend a whole day in this safe but exciting game. In distant parts, war-ravaged landscapes crumbled harmlessly away. Silently, thousands died. Oblivious to all else, one hardly noticed when a servant came to mend the fire or draw the curtains or ask for orders one was too preoccupied to give.

Did we ever think then, as we enjoyed these cosy hostilities, that one day a real war might come creeping up behind us, and suddenly, with a terrible day-of-judgment roar, obliterate our war of make-believe and ourselves and take all our possessions with it?

Why, Oh Why?

There is growing unease in informed circles at the Government's failure to consult those best qualified to advise it on the "war against terrorism". Why, for instance, has it not yet called on the veteran war hero, distinguished public servant and founder of the Royal Army Tailoring Corps, Lt Gen Sir Frederick ("Tiger") Nidgett to state his views?

Nidgett has immense experience in Middle East affairs. The man who, from his grimly held redoubt at Port Said, "defied the Nazi hordes battering and howling at the gates of Egypt in the dark days of 1942" (see his autobiography *Up Sticks and Away* (Viper and Bugloss, £18.99; paperback, £9.99; pp213-268) gained unrivalled insight into the Arab mind.

It has been said (*ibid*, pp298-313) that he could "pierce with gimlet eye through the tangled enigmatic beards of the sons of the desert to the dark reality within". His discovery that Arabic writing runs from right to left (*ibid*, pp165-179) proved to be "the catalyst for an expanding vista of original thinking".

Nidgett could not only see through tangled beards, but could tell one type of tangled beard from another, expertly distinguishing the Pashtun beard from the Tajik, the Uzbek from the Hazara.

It was a gift that stood him in good stead in his triumphant, textbook campaign against the Emir of Todi in the Fifties. And, again, it helped him in his brief but eventful term as Governor of Socotra in the Seventies, when his masterly handling of the problem of the island's infestation by legendary giant rocs earned him a formidable reputation throughout the Arab world.

"Tap a drum in Fez and its echo will be heard in Jakarta." This has always been Nidgett's guiding principle. It explains why, at this critical time, Nidgett's advice, fruit of a lifetime's experience, is worth more than the shallow musings of all your Hoons, Hains, Straws, Powells and Rumsfelds put together.

Above all, Nidgett believes, "we must build bridges with the average moderate terrorist. Without them, he will promptly shin up the proverbial gum tree like a dose of salts, spitting defiance at all and sundry. Engage him in dialogue, and he will be as putty in your hands".

On the Home Front

Residents of Kandahar Road, Jelalabad Avenue, Herat Drive, Mazar-i-Sharif Crescent and other roads in Nerdley laid out at the time of the 19th-century Afghan Wars have asked the council to change the names, because they are "too militaristic and politically offensive to the future broad-based, democratic government of Afghanistan".

They want "forward-looking" names, preferably those of statesmen who have distinguished themselves in the "war against terrorism", such as "General Hoon", as they call him, always a great favourite among Nerdley people. Other suggestions are "Long Haul Avenue", "Northern Alliance Road" and "Moderate Muslim Crescent", a subtle allusion to the well-known Muslim lunar symbol.

The troubled, embattled, beleaguered Stretchford United Football Club, now facing relegation from the Seventh Division, want to change the name of their fabled Anthrax Park ground, which is derelict and partly under water, to "something which will help the war effort". Suggestions are "Botulism Road" and "Bubonic Park".

Visual Images

The airborne travels of Tony Blair to the cities of the gorgeous East as he seeks support for his "anti-terrorist coalition" suggest to my mind's eye a whole series of my never-to-be painted historical paintings, already framed in dusty gilt and hanging in the seldom-visited Alderman Sugden Bequest Room at the Sowerby Bridge Municipal Museum and Art Gallery.

"Blair in the Pakistan" shows the sturdy, resolute leader quietly reading an improving chapter of the Koran to himself as before him a howling mob of Muslim enthusiasts brandishes staves, cudgels, rusting bicycle pumps and other weapons.

In "Blair Rebuffed by Saudis", we see him calm and resolute as he drinks green tea with sneering, white-robed sheikhs, with eunuch-guarded harems and oil wells in the background.

"Blair between Sharon and Arafat" is a composite study in which Blair, radiating impartiality and moral earnestness, still seems to quail as the two contrasting pantomime ogres bellow over his head. Finally, we have "Blair at the White House". Is there a hint of embarrassment on Bush's small, wooden face as he bids the kneeling Blair rise from his obeisance?

If Only

I told you how it would be. No sooner had Scottish devolution been set up — not necessarily bad in itself — than sure enough, the slyest, dullest, most verbiage-addicted, boring and priggish people in Scotland came creeping out of old newspaper articles and committee minutes to take it over.

Naturally these people wanted to ban foxhunting. Naturally they wanted to make it illegal for parents to smack their own badly behaved children. No doubt further measures are to come, compulsory lettuce-eating in schools, nuclear-free zones, fines for picking wild flowers, fines for drinking in public and singing "racist" football songs.

It is all the more galling because a worthy parliament for Scotland might be a splendid thing. It would be dominated, of course, by the great Scottish nobles and landowners, the Dukes of Atholl and Buccleuch and Montrose, casting a richly embroidered shadow of greatness over the necessary lawyers and accountants and suchlike.

A sense of history, of old unhappy, far-off things would pervade its deliberations. Even when it debated, as it sometimes must, housing and classroom sizes, the tragic aura of this small, brave, turbulent and gifted nation would preside. The old songs, fierce and melancholy, would linger always.

Nor would the noblemen and chieftains of Scotland scorn to sit in conclave beside distinguished figures of modern Scotland such as the odd football manager, adding a plangent note of eternal grievance and all too human woe, and reminding them, if reminder were needed, that they too were mortal.

A Famous Victory

No sooner had news of the fall of Kabul reached Stretchford than excited crowds spilt on to the streets, brandishing placards scrawled with badly spelt slogans: "Long Live the Northern Alliance!"; "Long Live the USAAF!"; "Kandahar or Bust!"; "Islamabad or Bust!"; "Washington or Bust!"

Typical housewives (some had dressed in hastily run-up burqas for the purpose of throwing them off), one world activists, lecturers on human rights, freelance technologists, bent fruit-machine mechanics, would-be television presenters, false mediums and soothsayers, ordinary British persons just released into the community — all the infinitely varied supporters and opponents of the "war against terrorism" and enthusiasts for a democratic, broad-based government for Afghanistan — all were there.

Disputes broke out, corresponding, as in a distorting mirror, to more sanguinary events in the far-off Hindu Kush.

Some argued about the respective merits of various warlords and their comparative expertise in the arts of rapine and murder. Some of the more linguistically ambitious shouted for General Mohammed Qasim Fahim, commander of the troops in the fabled Panjshir valley.

Some were for Ismail Khan, the "Lion of Herat". Some even favoured old Dr Burhanuddin Rabbani, still titular President of Afghanistan. But most yelled for General Abdul Rashid Dostum, believed to hold the record for the number of times he had changed sides since the Russians left. "Say what you like about General Dostum," said a typical student of Afghan affairs, "he's a man who knows his own mind, and just about as broad-based as you can get."

Rival fan clubs such as the Our General Abdul Rashid Dostum (and its corollary, the Our Anti-G.A.R.D.) were soon in being, promising an outsize headache for Det Supt J.B. Harrogate, the police fan club supremo. He is trying to form an amalgamated all-warlords' fan club, drawing all the fan clubs together, as he hopes, "into a broad-based discussion group, building bridges and initiating dialogue on a broad-based basis".

Broad-based

One of the most singular moves so far in the singular "war against terrorism" is the forthcoming UN conference in Bonn to which representatives of the various Afghan factions have been summoned to discuss a broad-based power-sharing government.

Will the delegates be taking their weapons with them? Will they be allowed to take them into the conference hall? Will they be inclined to use them to add force to their arguments? Will they understand that there will be no American bombers flying overhead to settle them?

The Taliban — even the strange creatures called the "moderate" Taliban — will be excluded from the conference. If, as seems likely, they are on the way out in Afghanistan itself, we are going to miss them. They have meant a great deal in the mysterious mythological cycle of the "war against terrorism". In fact it could hardly have done without them.

They are a thoroughly dislikeable lot, however. They are cruel and fanatical. In the One World Order of eternal peace and prosperity that Tony Blair orates about, there is no possible place for them. They hate dogs and music and drink and are rather strict about women. Yet it is said they hanged a television by the roadside as a warning to the people, so they can't be all bad.

On Standby

"The something that has happened is that the situation has changed so rapidly." In these eloquent words, Jack Straw, described as a Foreign Secretary, explained why British troops on standby had not yet been deployed. Did ever the voice of Britain ring out so loud and clear?

Meanwhile, it can be revealed, many more units may be put on standby. One of them is that grand old regiment the Royal Stretchfordshire Yeomanry, victors in a thousand glorious engagements from the indecisive Battle of Gnomesall Heath in the War of the Roses (1479) to the relief of Ormondroyd's Mill (1826), when they decisively repelled a five-man mob of Luddite rioters.

This regiment is also distinguished by the extreme complexity of its mess rituals which, as the present Adjutant, Capt J.R. St J. St X. Haggard-Jelkes, writes in his regimental history, "can only be likened to an elaborate version of the Kabbala and the Rulebook of the Amalgamated Holeborers' Union combined".

The present commanding officer, Lieut Col M.S.St V. St A. Lestrange-Haggard, is keen to lead his men to Afghanistan where, he believes, they "could make a vital contribution to securing a broad-based agreement". Threatened over the years by the machinations of malignant levellers in the Ministry of Defence, who have tried to amalgamate them with the 123rd Field Bakery Unit, they have learned to survive by cunning and backstairs intrigues, both of which should help them to deal with treacherous and bloodthirsty warlords.

Another fine body of men who could make an impact in Afghanistan is the Royal Army Tailoring Corps. Unfortunately it was disbanded some years ago. But the handpicked four-man team of ex-quartermasters who still run the holding unit on the site of a former dog biscuit factory at East Ardsley Junction in the West Riding could rapidly be reactivated to bring their own specialised experience to the hunt for bin Laden.

"We're mad keen and rarin' to go," says QMS (Lapels) John Numbe, echoing the RATC's great founder, Gen Sir Fredrick ("Tiger") Nidgett. "We reckon we could do a great job smartening up those Northern Alliance blokes. Let's face it, they're a right scruffy-looking shower, with their baggy trousers and their flowing robes all anyhow.

"They may be good soldiers, but they could do with a few trouser presses and button sticks and blanco to add those little touches that make all the difference on the battlefield and, even more, off it."

The American military are known to admire the special skills of the RATC, which have no parallel in their own armed forces. So what are we waiting for? Here is the chance for Tony Blair to gain the esteem of the USA as well as more glory for himself.

Party at Bonn

"Well Ahmed, who'd have thought of meeting you here?" "Who'd have thought of meeting you, Hamid? The last time I saw you, you were dealing with a batch of Taliban prisoners. What became of them?" "A slight misunderstanding, I'm afraid. I'm trying to get right out of the Middle Ages now." "Aren't we all?" "I say, Abdul, who on earth is that chap over there in the pin-striped suit?" "Must be one of the royalist lot from Rome."

"What are you doing with that Kalashnikov, Omar?" "We're supposed to leave our weapons in the cloakroom." "Evening, mullah. Glad to see you wearing your turban. Good to keep up the proper standards, eh?" "More mint tea, sir?" "Thank you, and I'll have a handful of those canapes too."

"Well, makes a change from Mazar-i-Sharif, eh?" "Yes, but I must say I find the grub here a bit odd, don't you?" "Too many Uzbeks here, if you ask me." "Can't stand Tajiks." "Can't stand Pashtuns." "And the same to you." "All right, all right. Keep your hair on. Where are we exactly, anyhow?" "I think we're in Germany." "Oh, I thought we were in Australia."

So goes the merry party chatter after the day's session of the UN conference. It will not be the last conference in the pleasant places of the earth where innumerable experts and officials meet to discuss how to lead the Afghan people into the world of the future. Meanwhile the Afghan people, scarcely comprehending, must struggle to live in the present, amid ruins that grow ever more extensive with the latest engines of destruction, under skies that rain down even more of the latest kinds of death.

Down the Mineshaft

Deep down in Deadwater leadmine (disused), near Bakewell in Derbyshire, Julian Birdbath, last citizen of the republic of letters, sat huddled over his rusting typewriter, while his pet toad, Amiel, his only friend, perched on his shoulder. He felt even less inclined than usual to work on his life of Stephen Spender.

Would it ever be finished, let alone published? What had the last letter from the Toadstone Press said? "In view of other books on Stephen Spender already published or in the pipeline, might not your own book be thought a work of supererogation?" There was also something about repaying his advance of £15.75.

In his mind's eye he saw the publisher, with his silly, pseudo-intellectual face and neat bow-tie, sitting in his office among the successful books on multicultural puppetry and corn dolly manufacture. Then he saw Spender himself, smugly addressing a conference in Tokyo on world peace and democracy. And the doomed writer gave a dismal groan to which his faithful toad joined a sympathetic croak.

He began musing on what he had read in a rain-sodden newspaper his neighbour Mr Shuttleworth had recently sent hurtling down the shaft. Yes, far away in Tora Bora, in the recesses of the White Mountains in Afghanistan, another rebel against the modern world sat in a splendidly appointed cavern impregnable to all assault and guarded by 400 warriors pledged to defend him with their lives.

Would he change places with Osama bin Laden, swap the typewriter for the gun, the dismal mineshaft for the well-appointed cavern, the life of a forgotten man of letters for the life of a terrorist beset by implacable enemies? Would bin Laden care to change places with him? Were both of them equally outcast and wandering in the wilderness of this world?

His head sank onto his typewriter, among the Spender papers sodden from the vapours of the mine. In a confused dream, Spender was reproving bin Laden for his indifference to world peace and democracy, while bin Laden, ignoring him, threatened the publisher with a portable rocket-launcher. Soon Birdbath's snores mingled with the crash of collapsing mining gear, the steady drip of stalactites and all the eerie noises that made up the strange symphony of the mine.

Tribute

Mary Whitehouse's long campaign for a bit of decency in television is over.

Often naive and aiming at the wrong targets, she did at least understand television's enormous, unprecedented power for evil and tried, vainly of course, to mitigate it. She might just as well have called for a total ban while she was about it.

By the mass of Left-wing thinkers, some of the most bigoted and unpersuadable people in England, this well-meaning woman was both mercilessly ridiculed and venomously hated. I have been told that her arch-enemy, the Great Bald Warthog Sir Hugh Greene, director-general of the BBC, who boasted he had made it "permissive", commissioned a life-sized oil painting of her in the nude, and would throw darts at it in leisure moments.

She might not have appreciated this. But what greater tribute could there be, coming from such a man, "of whom to be dispraised were no small praise"?

Double Vision

I have just had a cataract removed from my right eye — one of those triumphs of surgical technique that make one wonder whether there is not something to be said for certain kinds of scientific progress after all. Through my right eye I now see the world in its true colours again.

Through my left eye, on the other hand, which still has a cataract developing, I see the world as if through a dirty window. By closing one eye or the other, I command alternate worlds. My right eye gives me winter cold, bright and clear. My left eye gives me autumn, brown and gold as an old fading photograph.

The other day, looking idly at the world through my left eye only, I noticed that the world itself seemed to be different. Who was that man walking into the wood, dressed in a bygone style, wearing a trilby hat and whistling a music hall tune of a hundred years ago?

A horse-drawn cart passed slowly along the road. A woman in a bonnet, wheeling an old-fashioned bicycle in the other direction, stopped to talk to the driver. Apart from their faint voices there was not a sound. Not even a single primitive biplane marred the silence of the sky. It was a tranquil scene in an England where King Edward had just begun to reign.

I switched eyes and saw the familiar world and heard the familiar mechanical uproar of this disastrous millennial year. It was just as well I did. That other scene might soon become addictive, then inescapable. And what would happen then?

Year Ending

Of all the disasters of this first millennial year, it is not the destruction of the World Trade Centre, with the consequent "war against terrorism", that comes home to me the most.

It is a disaster not celebrated with windy rhetoric and public ceremonies. Amid all the vainglorious talk of endless war for universal righteousness, it is hardly mentioned.

It is the plague of foot and mouth, which has devastated the country districts of England, brought about the slaughter of millions of innocent animals and reduced whole communities — and those some of the best people in England — to ruin and despair.

It has fallen upon what to me is the best-loved of all places in England, the Eden Valley, changing forever what seemed unchangeable. All summer, day after day, I read of the ruin that had come upon Reagill and Kirkoswald, on Appleby and Kirkby Stephen, on Orton and Crosby Ravensworth, familiar name after name.

It was a plague mysterious in its origin and mismanaged in its progress by a government which concealed its doings either because it did not know what it was doing from one moment to the next or because it was engaged, as some think, in a conspiracy to eliminate people like the farmers of Westmorland who stand in the way of the coming totalitarian state.

It is this, rather than global trumpetings, that should concern us here in England now.

Christmas Treat

Sir Aylwin Goth-Jones, the genial, unpopular chief constable of Stretchford, is looking forward to his best "drink-drive season" — his term for Christmas — for many years.

Apart from a few officers doing surveillance on possible "race-related" incidents, he has mobilised his whole force for the Christmas "drink-drive" campaign.

To the delight of all, the new helicopters have arrived. With good management it should be possible to keep three or four of them buzzing and rattling in the Stretchford skies at all times.

Although of the latest type, it is disappointing that they are not armed with machine-guns and rocket-launchers like "proper helicopter gunships". But, as Sir Aylwin tells his "lads" soothingly, it will all come in time.

A great joy is a new system by which all who come to the police with information about "drink-drivers" get rewards. The most encouraging thing, Sir Aylwin says, is that crowds of children are bringing information about their parents to get rewards of sweets, mince pies, pop records and condoms.

"I met one happy little girl — couldn't be more than six — who told me that her mum and dad were planning a Christmas party 'with lots of drinks, and I'm sure that they and their friends mean to drive. I can tell, you know, by the daft expression in their eyes.'

"I almost had tears in my own eyes," says Sir Aylwin, beaming, "thinking of the model citizen that little girl is going to be. And, you know, there are thousands like her. This year I'm hoping to get double the number of drivers stopped on the road over last year's figures. Even if the number of actual convictions is unfortunately down, I feel it is going to be our best drink-drive season ever!"

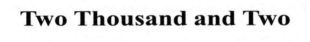

Two Thousand and Two

Tidings of Joy

By *Mungo Clange*

Were you there among the crowd at Heathrow the other day (as I was), when Tony and Cherie Blair set off on their mission to bring peace to Papua New Guinea, where stone-age tribes in the remote mountains, long at odds, are on the verge of open war? The Blairs have already brought peace to Northern Ireland and Afghanistan. They have settled the dispute between India and Pakistan. Now they seek to solve a smaller problem indeed, but one which in our global world is just as vital.

In the vast waiting crowd, every strand of our multiracial society was represented. There were pale-faced earnest workers from the great Midlands call centres, keen-eyed Indian and Pakistani shopkeepers, each wielding a picturesque abacus, as well as smiling Afro-Caribbean rappers, gaily dressed Tanzanians with their gongs and cymbals, Romanians and Albanians, even the odd Eskimo, not to speak of innumerable ordinary, average Britons just released into the community.

All of us were tense with expectation. Suddenly a great cheer went up. The Blairs had been sighted on a distant runway, reported a man with a powerful telescope, just as they were about to board their plane. Fully prepared for this new mission, Mr Blair, that man of many pivots, was carrying a stone axe, while Cherie already had her face painted with elaborate designs in red and ochre and was wearing several nose rings and a many-stranded necklace of telephone wire which enhanced her long, graceful neck.

At the thought of their pivotal power for good, one of the biggest lumps I have ever known came into my throat. I must have passed out for a moment. "You all right, sir?" A typical, handsome young bobby had pulled me to my feet and was shaking me, not unpleasurably, as he went through the traditional routine of "feeling my collar". There was an intriguing jingle of handcuffs. "More than all right, officer," I said. "Aren't we all?" With a playful jab of his notebook in my ribs and a cheerful "no charge this time", he strode away.

A little grey-haired old lady dabbed my eyes with a wisp of lace redolent of old-world lavender gardens. "There, that's better. Tony and Cherie are real pivots for all seasons, aren't they?" she whispered. A typical Irish building worker, with a sprig of shamrock behind his ear and a UNO medallion bouncing on his bare chest, deftly produced an Irish stew from his big red spotted handkerchief and shared it amongst us. A group of Chelsea pensioners, ramrod-straight, came marching past. The distant chimes of Big Ben mingled with the clip-clop of Life Guards' horses.

In a sudden hush, somewhere in the crowd a single donkey brayed.

Quaking Ground

Overt anti-Semitism is said to be on the increase in this country. What is anti-Semitism? It ranges all the way from the total, world-historical anti-Semitism of the Nazis, by which the Jews were seen as enemies of the human race who must therefore be exterminated, to the casual, vulgar anti-Semitism everybody knows. But every kind of anti-Semitism springs consciously or unconsciously from the perception that the Jewish people is not as other peoples are.

Whether or not divinely chosen, its persistence as a distinct people from ancient times to the present day is a unique historical phenomenon so astounding and mysterious that it must surely give the most bigoted rationalist pause to think. The State of Israel, established in fulfilment of an ancient prophecy, is like no other state. Its absolute "right to exist" is a claim made by no other state in the world. It is now unmistakably at the centre of everything that is happening in the world and everything that is going to happen.

But such is the horror aroused by centuries of persecution and mass murder that even to discuss these matters openly, even to suggest that the Jews have an immense influence in the world for good and ill, may be denounced as "anti-Semitism" and therefore inadmissible. With the steady growth of thought control, it may even become illegal. Can this be a good thing for anybody?

On the Ohm Farm

"Aye, an' nobbut time too, look you," growled old Seth Roentgen, Britain's greatest agrotechnological farmer, flinging himself back in his gnarled old rocking chair and waving an even more gnarled forefinger. He is one of the last remaining speakers of the Old British Composite Dialect and is paid a handsome subsidy by English Heritage for speaking it to tourists.

He was talking about a new plan drawn up by Defra, by which every farmer in the land will have a computer linked to Whitehall. Every farmer will have to draw up a "business plan" which will be lodged electronically with Defra, enabling it to enforce obedience to all ministerial decrees and regulations.

"That's t' stuff to give 'em!" he crowed, calling up his own "e-enabled farm plan" on the gigantic screen that dominates his combined parlour and control room, low-raftered and hung with horse brasses, pewter pots, video tape-recorders and warming pans. Lovingly he checked the total assets of the Ohm Farm — soil, stock, crops and machinery — noting with particular pride that it contained not a single tree, plant or wild creature whatsoever.

"Indeed to goodness, at Ohm Farm us'n been all set to meet Defra's requirements lang syne," he chuckled. "As for they pesky wold small farmers, they be right dumboozled in thikky day and age. In a few years we'll see the back of them althegither. Good riddance to bad rubbish! Can't stop progress. Can't put t'clock back," he shouted in an exultant frenzy. "No, bah gum, begorrah, hoots awa', look you!"

For the People

Repeatedly sacked by vandals, a rendez-vous for the unlicensed vendors of obscene glass paperweights, reportedly haunted by ghosts of bygone referees and subject to subsidence from mine workings, the National Kids' Museum of Multicultural Football Excellence, opened with great eclat by Dr Spaceley-Trellis, the go-ahead Bishop of Stretchford, only two years ago, is to be merged with StretchMod, the sensationally  successful Museum of Modern Art which has already attracted more than three million visitors this year.

"We shall incorporate a combined football and kids' theme in the now enlarged gallery," says Sir Howard Dreadberg, director of StretchMod. "Hopefully we shall declare, develop and enable a dynamic symbiosis of art, youth and football for today and tomorrow."

Mystery Intruder

When Abdul Rashid Mahmud, otherwise Stan Horrocks, 29, of no fixed address, appeared at Nerdley magistrates court accused of loitering in suspicious circumstances and assaulting the police, he refused to recognise the court.

In evidence, Det Sgt J.B. Mackenzie, 38, of Nerdley Special Branch, said he was proceeding along Kandahar Road on January 12, on a routine search, when he observed the accused hastily assuming a false beard and a "Taliban-type" turban and adopting an "aggressive, defiant stance".

When he (Sgt Mackenzie) asked what he was doing, the accused stated that he was a prominent terrorist, a member of Spagbollah, an extremist wing of the Taliban, sworn to liberate first Nerdley from the infidel, then the whole Stretchford conurbation, then the whole world.

Cautioned, he stated: "Why don't you join us, copper, instead of being a uniformed stooge of the infidel and therefore doomed to hell fire?" He described the rewards he (Sgt Mackenzie) might expect in Paradise, including an unlimited supply of virgins and sherbet in a range of flavours. Flapping his arms excitedly, he struck him (Sgt Mackenzie) a violent blow on the chest, causing minor damage to the notebook and ballpoint pen.

He (Sgt Mackenzie) then arrested him. At the station he demanded that Dr F.S. Iftikarullah, Grand Mufti of Stretchford, be sent for. When this was refused, he lapsed into a torpor.

Dr F. Gestaltvogel, chief consultant psychiatrist at St Bogwena's General Hospital, said that ever since Islam had been so much in the news, "I am meeting such cases every day in my clinic". Examining Mahmud, he had shown him an Arabic copy of the Koran, but his only comment was "it seems to be in funny writing". He recommended a course of abreactive treatment, in which the patient would be shown alternate photographs of ferocious, black-turbaned Taliban warriors and equally ferocious red-faced, gum-chewing American prison guards.

Binding Mahmud over, Dr Ellis Goth-Jones, 61, the chairman, said that unfortunately he had no power to make an example of him by shaving his false beard, putting him in chains and handing him over to the American authorities as an unlicensed combatant. He believed that moderate Muslims had much to contribute to the rich tapestry of our multicultural society. As for Muslim extremists, he did not think more leisure facilities in the shape of artificial ski-runs and bowling alleys were necessarily the answer.

Well Done!

Three heroic Cornishmen, members of the ancient Stannary parliament, have been asserting Cornish national identity by removing English Heritage signs from historic places such as King Arthur's Castle at Tintagel. They have set a fine example to Englishmen, for whom these emblems of the heritage industry should be equally abhorrent, for different reasons.

Wherever they are — and they spring up like rank weeds, indicating anything from an ancient manor house to Old Seth Roentgen's Kids' Holiday Farm — these ugly brown objects serve to encourage the odious tourist industry, and worse, are pernicious signs of creeping socialism.

The socialist state, intent on total control, seeks to rule even over human curiosity and desire for knowledge. Nobody must be allowed to admire or discover anything for himself. All must be supplied with statutory parcels of knowledge and learn what they are told, so that all may be, in this way too, useful subjects of the state.

Exciting

Following the example of Humberside police, Stretchford police have appointed a poet-in-residence, Claude Goth-Jones, who will accompany officers on the beat. They have also appointed a conceptual artist-in-residence, Barry Goth-Jones, a conceptual potter-in-residence, Linda Goth-Jones, who will operate a portable kiln and potter's wheel on the beat, Giselle Goth-Jones, a conceptual fashion designer-in-residence, and Waldo Goth-Jones, a conceptual musician-in-residence, who will play the miniature clavichord, didgeridoo and Papuan linoleum harp.

They are all part of the dynamic Chief Constable Sir Alwyn Goth-Jones's plans for "building bridges between the police and the arts and emphasising their ongoing key role in an informed, democratic society". Not all policemen agree, however. Some think the presence of "dozens of arty-tarty weirdos on the beat will undermine police morale and encourage criminals to commit offences while the police are distracted by music, fashion parades and discussions on art history".

The public are not altogether happy either. "I know we've got to build ongoing bridges between the police and the community and the arts and everything," says Trish McElbow, 42, a multiple mother and freelance pawnbroker, of Sebastopol Road, Nerdley. "But will all these people have powers of arrest? If so, it will be worse than the Taliban."

Sir Alwyn is scornful of these objections. "There are bound to be teething troubles with any imaginative, exciting new concept," he says. "And there will always be people who are afraid of creative innovation and change. But I look forward to a time when policing itself will be a form of conceptual art, without anybody being arrested or any unpleasantness of that sort."

Missing

In the calendar of the New World Order, the list of sacred days is mounting up. Holocaust Memorial Day is already established. September the Eleventh Memorial Day will soon be there. But there is no memorial day for the millions of victims of that festival of slaughter, rape and pillage, the Red Army's invasion and conquest of Eastern Europe in 1945.

There is no proposal, either, for a general memorial day for all the victims of Communism in Russia, in China and throughout the world, far more numerous than all the victims of all the other tyrannical systems put together. What would be a suitable day for such a memorial? Karl Marx's birthday?

You may well ask why no such memorial is likely to join the list; and then ask again.

Unforgotten

In April the 70th anniversary of the "mass trespass" on Kinder Scout, the highest point of the Derbyshire Peak, will be celebrated with great enthusiasm by the Ramblers' Association and even by the National Trust, which now owns the site.

The organisers of the trespass were Communist activists from Manchester. Their purpose was not only to assert their "right to roam" over private property, but also their doctrinaire opposition to private property altogether. In the event, about 400 of these people and their followers invaded Kinder Scout, then privately owned, beat off a few gamekeepers and triumphantly occupied the summit.

Four of the ringleaders were sent to prison for riotous assembly and incitement to violence. They became heroes and martyrs for the ramblers' movement and an inspiration for the political drive against private property embodied in the infamous "right to roam" legislation of the Blairite Government.

There is a bronze plaque commemorating the affair in the National Trust car park at the start of the pathway to Kinder Scout.

In a remote region of this column there is a wide expanse of moorland very like the Peak, part of a nobleman's estates, where no rambler's foot has ever trod. No foaming radical or smug class warrior has ever set greedy eyes on it. No signposts or information boards direct the too many to its secret recesses.

No team of bureaucrats have declared it an area of outstanding natural beauty or a site of special scientific interest or classified its "landscape value" on their prosaic scale. No scientist has peeped and botanised upon it, or fenced it off for nature reserves and eco-habitats.

Here we have raised in our hearts a memorial stone with an inscription in Latin and English, dedicated to the memory of those anonymous gamekeepers, those humble, inarticulate men who bravely withstood the Red mob, defending, perhaps unknowingly, one of the great principles of human freedom, the right to private property.

Musical Offering

According to Norman Lebrecht, an American musician is "illuminating" Mahler's music by fusing it with jazz and Jewish themes and using Chinese and electric instruments. The old Stretchford Municipal Symphony Orchestra (it disappeared in the cultural revolution of 1992 when the council's arts committee withdrew its grant of £200 a year and turned the Sadcake Hall into a National Centre for Rap Excellence) had to do something like this, but from necessity.

Most of their instruments were decayed and mouldering, and they had to carry out running repairs even during performances, here substituting an outsized rubber band for a missing cello string, here a crown cork for a bassoon key, here a lump of dried mashed potato for a trombone mute.

To supplement their starvation wages, they carried on minor trades under cover of the music. Miss Hilda Craggs, the principal harpist, for many years kept a sewing machine behind her harp, using pedals and treadle as required with remarkable skill. Jim Moronowicz, a double bass, had a hot dog stand on the platform.

The percussion players regularly did minor car repairs, including respraying and tyre retreads. By blending the various noises of their trades

— clanging, hissing, frying, hammering — with Mahler's score, they made his already rich and elaborate orchestration even richer and more elaborate.

Their veteran conductor, Sir Jim Gastropodi, who was hard of hearing as well as shortsighted and subject to strange fits of absence, combined a passionate love of Mahler with a warm indulgence towards his "lads" in a positive steamed treacle pudding of sentiment. He felt that Mahler might not entirely approve, but would be inclined to give them the benefit of the doubt.

Music critics were dubious. But no one who heard the SMSO's version of the three-hour slow movement of the Forty Third Symphony (the "Interminable") — at once doom-laden yet sarcastic, tender yet strident, solemn yet hilarious, calm yet hysterical — will ever forget it.

Justice

On the first day of the show trial of Slobodan Milosevic at The Hague, Carla Del Ponte, chief prosecutor of the United Nations International Criminal Tribunal for the former Yugoslavia, spoke of the "medieval savagery" of the "war crimes" he is alleged to have ordered or failed to stop. For those who work for that mysterious entity, the "International Community", and gather at the Bar of World Opinion, the word "medieval" is a common term of abuse.

Is medieval savagery, perpetuated by identifiable people caught up in the bloodthirsty frenzy of civil war, worse than modern savagery, in which people are targeted by mathematical calculation and blown to bits by bombs dropped from a height of 50,000 feet by anonymous airmen?

If Milosevic is guilty of "war crimes", although he may have personally killed no one, what about Clinton, Blair and others responsible for the shameful and treacherous war against the Serbs in 1999? When will they be brought to trial at The Hague?

The "international justice" Del Ponte speaks of so smugly is a parody of justice. It is a manoeuvre dressed up in fine words, for furtherance of the "One World" policies of the "International Community". Only those who have somehow got in the way of those policies will ever risk being brought to trial. Others can commit acts of medieval, modern or future savagery as they please and still go free.

Then and Now

"Sanctions are beginning to bite." Now that sanctions are again imposed on the country once called Rhodesia, that parrot cry from Harold Wilson's time is echoing in my mind. It is all ancient history now. Who remembers the days of 30 years ago, when the Rhodesians, heroic in their unheroic plainness, stood alone, still undefeated, against a world of lies? Who remembers how Jeremy Thorpe and the legions of Hampstead thinkers bravely called for the bombing of Rhodesia? How the "Beira Patrol", celebrated in many a stirring, salt-caked liberal legend of the sea, vainly strove to block the passage of supplies to Rhodesia by wicked "sanctions busters" through the Portuguese colony of Mozambique?

Those sanctions never bit anybody at all. The resourceful Rhodesians took to manufacturing their own essential goods with great success. Will the present sanctions against Mugabe bite more deeply? Whereas the sanctions against the Rhodesians were intended to starve them out, those against Mugabe seem designed mainly to prevent him from visiting London and staying in his usual suite at Claridge's. Can a "Mayfair patrol" of seconded policemen and traffic wardens keep him out?

Seen at a distance of 30 years, the Rhodesians' achievement in holding out so long against such odds seems even more remarkable and even more admirable than it did then. The policy of our own government seems even more shameful. In 1980, after sham elections hardly more "fair and free" from intimidation than Mugabe's elections are likely to be, the deed was done. A country prosperous and well governed enough was handed over to that hero of Hampstead and symbol of Western self-laceration, "Bob" Mugabe, and in due course succumbed to savagery and confusion. No word of protest was then heard. No contrite word is heard now from those who approved and carried out that base act of surrender.

Correspondence

Sir — May I add my own small tribute to the late Sir Walter Winterbottom, rightly regarded as the finest footballing mind England has ever produced? In the far-off days of the 1950s I worked as an archivist in the historical section of the Football Association at Lancaster Gate, under the all-seeing eye of Dr (later Sir) Stanley Rous, himself the possessor of a first-class footballing mind.

I well remember the daily conferences where questions of coaching, tactics, training, selection of players for the England team and other matters of that ilk were debated in an atmosphere of intellectual pyrotechnics which would have amazed and humbled the average fellow of All Souls.

Rous and Winterbottom did not always see eye to eye. On one occasion, I remember, Winterbottom was arguing with his usual brilliance that a knowledge of calculus and Boolean algebra was essential for a good goalkeeper. Rous disputed this, holding that a knowledge of trigonometry and conic sections was enough. The argument got so heated that Rous, who was notorious for his "short fuse", suddenly banged down his cherished first edition of Newton's *Principia Mathematica* on the table and stormed out of the room.

Soon we felt the whole building shaking as he pounded out a mighty Bach toccata on the five-manual organ he had installed in his private apartments to soothe him at times of stress. It was paid for, as I recall, by the subscriptions of hundreds of loyal retired footballers of that ilk.

Dudley Register,
Gnomesall Heath, Staffs

The Last Enemy

A recent speech by President Bush to a gathering of more than 100,000 veterans and their families at Grand Rapids, Montana, has had remarkably little notice in this country. Unfortunately I cannot print it in full. But this abridgement, I think, gives the gist of the President's thinking:

"Fellow Americans, I want to talk to you today about a new and deadly menace to our country: the menace of Terroristan. That is a country many of you may not have heard of. We do not yet know precisely where it is located. But we do know that it is the ultimate focus of evil. It is the apogee of evil. It is the meridian and zenith of evil. It is the hypotenuse of evil. We are going to deal with this evil country with all the resources at our command.

"But first we are going to find out where Terroristan is — wherever it is. It may be in Asia. It may be in Europe. It may be in Africa or South America or Australia. It may be at the North Pole or at the South Pole. It may be way up in the stratosphere.

"Wherever it is, we are going to go after it and find it. Wherever it may be lurking on the map of the world or outside it, we're going to find it, dead or alive, and then make sure it is dead.

"Only when we have taken out Terroristan can we be sure of permanent peace and security for our country. And, though that may be a lesser matter, peace and security for the whole world. I ask you, with complete confidence, men, women, children, grandchildren and great grandchildren of America, to give me your unwavering support in this great endeavour."

Memories of Yore

Memories of life in the Football Association's headquarters at Lancaster Gate in the early Fifties have drawn thousands of angry letters, many of them written in purple and green ink on the back of pieces of wallpaper and gnawed at the edges.

One of these, from "an old time football administrator", calls our account "gratuitously and perversely misleading. For a kick-off (if I may use this expression) Walter Winterbottom's disagreement with Sir Stanley Rous on the occasion mentioned had nothing whatever to do, I recall, with the need for goalkeepers to have a good knowledge of higher mathematics. On that, both men were agreed.

"The argument was about Winterbottom's highly original plan for an England forward line of 10 players, with defence left entirely to the goalkeeper. Sir Stanley, in my view, would never have relieved his feelings by playing a Bach toccata on the organ in his private apartments. On one such occasion, when he lost his temper, I recall, he gave a tremendous performance, causing a chimney stack to collapse, of his own composition, *Ketelbeyana*, in which *In a Monastery Garden*, *In a Persian Market*, *In a Dentists' Waiting Room* and other well-known tone poems were incorporated in a brilliant contrapuntal fantasia.

"It was subsequently arranged for brass band by Rimmer, and played, I believe, at the 1950 Cup Final. Need I say more?

Get Fell In

The Army is to allow soldiers' girlfriends to spend nights with them in barracks. It may also set up "welfare houses" where soldiers can hire rooms for their girlfriends and even take in alcohol, "where deemed appropriate". This is all part of a drive to get rid of "barrack room culture" and drag the Army kicking and screaming, as the saying is, into the 21st century.

Far from bringing more freedom, it may turn out to be part of the 21st century's tendency to regulate and control every detail of our lives. Soldiers who would have used their own initiative in such matters and made their own arrangements will find their amours and alcohol intake tabulated and organised. "Can't bring that bird in here, mate. Where's your G1076 form for authorisation?"

"Barrack room culture" will change into "Civvy Street Culture", with all the horrors of "relationship problems", "emotional literacy", compulsory "safe sex" and unlimited rivalry, jealousy and indiscipline. Barrack room lawyers and professional counsellors will be everywhere. And the last state will be worst than the first.

But Dr Heinz Kiosk, the eminent social psychologist and chief psychiatric adviser to the Barrack Room Furniture Authority, takes a different view. "Bringing the Army into the 21st century is long overdue. However, outdated attitudes, sexism, homophobia and other old-fashioned prejudices may still linger.

"It is vital that women soldiers should have an equal right to bring their boyfriends into barracks. Gays of both genders should have the same rights. And the needs of fetishists of all kinds will have to be met. Some of these, the bondage community and the leather folk, for example, may require elaborate and expensive equipment.

"I am sure taxpayers will not grudge this. It will ensure that at last we have an army that has outgrown unenlightened, patriarchal attitudes and is fully equipped for the 21st century, both for peacekeeping operations and even for so-called 'military' operations, if any."

African Dreams

There is nothing surprising about Mr Mugabe's victory. What is surprising is that he bothers about elections at all. There must be easier ways of holding on to power than beating up voters, stuffing ballot boxes with fake papers and losing them or setting them on fire, and generally rigging the result.

And for all the shock, horror and distress among Western liberal thinkers, there is nothing surprising about the African countries' support for him. The quarrel in Zimbabwe, as in all of Africa, is between the white man and the black man. The black man, as Mugabe knows and the white thinker denies, would like to get rid of the white man and all the white man's laws and institutions that linger on so confusingly from colonial times and irritate Mugabe and his fellow potentates by getting in the way.

There is an obvious remedy. Let the black man get rid of the white man's democratic elections, his parliaments and woolsacks and judges' wigs, his military uniforms, his weapons and other ingenious devices, his science and technology, his money and financial arrangements, his motor cars and aircraft, his computers, radio and television, not to speak of his hospitals and medical services.

No longer ensnared by the white man's overpowering gifts, the Africans could return to African ways of doing things. The African chief would summon his tribal council and dispense African justice. Wars would be fought with sticks and stones. Cattle would be currency. Witch doctors would flourish with their spells and potions.

The people would dance and sing and celebrate birth and death and the procession of the seasons. The fat man, reclining in the shade, would have the thin men scurrying about to do his bidding, as from time immemorial.

No news, good or bad, would come out of Africa any more to fill our "media" with worry and soul-searching. Experts and liberal thinkers, deprived of conscience-fodder and obsessive guilt, would have to find other ways of passing their time. And Africa, free of mad, white, alien dreams of progress and modernity, would be itself again.

Lost Cause

The voice of democracy and modernity has spoken. If foxhunting survives at all, it will be as "pest control", under licence, part of the apparatus of the Blairite total state, the dim wraith of the living glory it has been. It will be subject to bureaucratic regulations and overseen by officials who will want to squeeze even its pathetic remnants out of existence.

So all that courage and beauty and skill, all that well-loved custom and ritual, all that conviviality of country people, must fall victim to the vicious spite of foaming Leftists and liberal prigs filled with hatred of their betters, helped by deluded animal lovers who do not understand what company they are in.

How could that epitome of old ways of living survive in England now? It is a country where what is worst is admired and encouraged, and what is best is derided and condemned; where vile entertainment is an addiction for its brainwashed citizens; where an alien and degenerate "youth culture" daily spreads its poison among the innocent; where a creeping publisher can hail moronic West Indian doggerel as classic poetry; where money not merely rules but is officially deified.

Foxhunting has come out of the human past when England was still England. Its cause is lost. But foxhunting people should still fight on. What decent man would not fight for a good cause because he knew it was a lost one? It is no great consolation to reflect that the proud Blairite state itself, with all its smug certainties, its arrogant apparatus of conformity, will one day perish too as though it had never been.

In Sadcake Park

In lovely, sex maniac-haunted Sadcake Park, Stretchford's "iron lung", as elsewhere, spring has come. Along the paths among the regimented flower beds, with their lurid patterns of marigolds, pink and yellow and magenta, the maniacs walk warily, eyed by brown-uniformed park attendants of pseudo-military bearing.

One maniac, convulsively gripping the right cuff of his long mackintosh, proceeds with short, mincing steps towards the cafeteria by the boating-lake, wheeling a rusting bicycle with a basket on its handlebars. It contains an assortment of objects: a broken barometer, a mildewed, green, gleaming euphonium, a toy rabbit with flopping ears, an outsize pork pie.

Glaring from his collapsing hut, Mr Bloth, the keeper of the boats, disgustedly surveys the lake, rich with chemical pollutants and debris: supermarket trolleys, tins, bottles and chewed cardboard from the cafeteria, and a relic from some bankrupt garden centre, part of a concrete effigy of Hercules and the Nemean Lion.

Across the water, on his island of artificial stone, Mr R.S. Viswaswami, thought to be the only naked sadhu employed by a British local government authority, reclines in his wall-to-wall carpeted grotto on cushions embroidered by pious Hindu women.

Idly, he projects a small thought-form, an apsara or nymph, who dances with sinuous gestures on the water, then vanishes with a tinkling laugh. Bloth, his old enemy, who is an environmental officer of lower rank, groans with dismal lust, wondering what thought-form the fat black bastard will project to tease him further.

He shakes his fist. But the sadhu, now well into his stride, projects a whole series: a Himalayan storm with purple lightning; early morning mass teeth-brushing at Sealdah Station, Calcutta, and a stampede of elephants which makes the sex maniacs run, hooting in panic, to hide pointlessly under bare municipal boughs.

Urgent

The news that two lumps of ice as big as Somerset and half Cyprus respectively, have broken off the Antarctic ice-field has immensely excited glaciologists, meteorologists, climatologists and other experts in their hundreds of thousands throughout the world. The massed cheering of the global warming community is enough to loosen a lump of ice the size of Mongolia and set it drifting menacingly in the southern ocean.

Dr Ron Hardware, who heads a dedicated team of research scientists at Nerdley University, is also on the alert. "In our search for a unified field theory of human ills," he says, "we've already found probable links between passive smoking and cancer, Alzheimer's disease and multiple sclerosis, as well as moral plagues like racism, sexism, homophobia, Toryism, cot death and drink-driving. Is there a link between all these and global warming?

"Preliminary research strongly suggests that there is. But as yet we know all too little of the linking factors. We need to do a great deal more research. And for that we need more research workers, more facilities and above all, more money. We need, in short, a government crash programme with funding in the millions. It is not much to ask. It is disgraceful that a government which prides itself on supporting science should be slow to help us. Do they want British scientists to be the laughing stock of the world?"

What the Papers Say

In a thoughtful leader, the *Feudal Times and Reactionary Herald* discusses the proposed ban on foxhunting: "Many of our readers are foxhunters; almost all of them, we trust, will have followed the hunt at one time. We have been struck by the great number of letters we have received on this issue from those who seldom put pen to paper.

"Unanimous in their condemnation, they differ on how to deal with this upsurge of the most contemptible and odious among Her Majesty's subjects — superannuated schoolteachers, ignorant and brutalised ruffians and partisans of the so-called Labour faction (which has no more to do with honest labour, of course, than the so-called Conservative faction has to do with conserving anything worthwhile).

"Some recommend hanging for these people; others favour smoking them out of their malodorous dens and turning them loose, as one eloquent letter puts it, to wander the world and beg for their bread in desolate places. While fully sharing their indignation, we would recommend wiser counsels, such as a mass march on Parliament which would compel MPs to rescind their disgusting Bill on pain of being tied in sacks and flung into the Thames.

"But if the Bill, in spite of everything, should actually pass through both Houses of Parliament, there is still one last resort. The Royal Assent, without which it cannot become law, might be withheld. We do not usually take it upon ourselves to offer advice to Her Majesty. But in a matter of such crucial importance, we venture to do so.

"It may be that, in the event of her refusing her assent to this infamous measure, the republican mob, daily growing more insolent, would seize the pretext to force her abdication. So be it. There can be no better issue than this on which to precipitate such a cataclysmic event.

"Foxhunting, though not all of our readers will agree, is something more than foxhunting. It is a symbol of all that remains of Old England. With it stands or falls the hereditary principle, indeed the monarchy itself. A threat to end the monarchy in such a way could not but rivet the minds of millions and send such a warning to this realm, nay, to the whole world, that the campaign against foxhunting would collapse amid universal execration and derision."

Glory

They say that Paddy Ashdown, the great Liberal leader, is to be given high office in Bosnia, as governor, no less. It will not be long, we monarchists all hope, before he is offered the crown and ascends the throne of Bosnia as King Paddy the First. The last king of Bosnia, Steven VII Tomasevic, surrendered to the Turks and was beheaded in 1463. But times have changed, and this should not necessarily be a precedent.

Approached by a joint delegation of the Serb, Croat and Muslim communities, he will at first pretend to put the crown aside, then yield to their urgent pleas. How glorious, when in Sarajevo, at a ceremony with specially devised ecumenical rites (Catholic, Greek Orthodox, Muslim, Methodist, agnostic, humanist, Salvation Army), the Secretary-General of the United Nations, Kofi Annan himself, places the crown on his head.

Loud the people's acclamations, loud the pealing organs and massed choirs with all the bells of Sarajevo ringing out as leaders of the three communities swear allegiance! Later, he inspects a guard of honour of the happily named Nato Dissuasion Force, then tours the city.

His piercing blue eyes, screwed up with almost intolerable sincerity, scan the remotest forests and reactionary mountains for signs of emerging liberalism. Peasants in their picturesque costumes have trooped in from the countryside, bearing traditional gifts: ornamental daggers, pots of honey, embroidered shawls, clotted cream and new-laid eggs.

Folk songs mingle with the strains of "He's A Jolly Good Fellow", "Follow The Van" and (an allusion to the new monarch's Irish ancestry) "If You're Irish, Come Into The Parlour". Helicopter gunships and squadrons of fighter aircraft fly past as the King chats easily to his people. They laugh heartily at well-chosen anecdotes of his time as Liberal leader. Distant explosions mark pockets of resistance, to be mopped up by the Bosnian army. He orders the search for "war criminals" — slab-faced Mladic and tousle-headed Karadzic — to be intensified.

As night falls, dense fumes of slivovitz hang over the sleeping city. A sound of massed snoring comes from the Royal Palace, where King Paddy sits at ease, regaling his courtiers with extracts from his Liberal party conference speeches and statements of liberal ideals: the need for dialogue and for a determined but carefully considered step forward into the future.

An Odd Incident

For many years the Queen Mother was a frequent guest at Simpleham. We always looked forward to her visits and enjoyed our talks about racing and her hilarious anecdotes of meetings with T.S. Eliot, Stephen Spender, Dylan Thomas and other literary friends.

I remember one curious incident in, I think, 1974. We were having drinks on the South Terrace and talking of this and that when a footman, Hitchens I think it was, appeared and told me that "a person calling himself Woodrow Wyatt" had called, claiming to be "a friend of Her Majesty".

This was so manifestly absurd that I told Hitchens to show the insolent fellow the door. "Use the minimum of force," I said. "If he gives any trouble, get Prentice to help you."

I heard later that the two footmen rather exceeded their instructions. When Wyatt started to bluster and tried to bribe them with cigars and promises of "top jobs in Fleet Street", they took him to a remote part of the West Wing and stuffed him under a billiard table. He had to be released with block and tackle. Later on, I believe, he was made a "life peer", which seemed entirely suitable.

Peace Process

"I mean what I say," said President Bush, not once but several times, admonishing stiff-necked Sharon and, for good measure, poor old Arafat. So speaks a schoolmaster who can't keep order in the class. "If you don't stop that noise, I don't know what I shall do."

So, in their different ways, speak the innumerable politicians and pontificators who continually call on Israelis and Palestinians alike to stop that dreadful noise and be reasonable, start a peace process, any old kind of peace process, agree to set up two states, Israeli and Palestinian, which will co-exist in perpetual peace and guarantee the right of Israel to exist.

But whatever Bush and Blair and the rest of them think, the world is not reasonable. The existence of Israel itself, a unique kind of state based on an ancient prophecy and an eternal wrong, is not reasonable. Its right to exist, which the Arabs will never accept, rests not on reasonable arguments but on its own ability to fight for its existence by any means available, however distasteful this may seem to the "international community".

Not reason, but ancient elemental forces, racial and historical memories, even traces of that romantic revolt against reason sometimes called fascism are working here, and on both sides. When Sharon looks in the glass, does he see a man of reason, keen on human rights and racial equality and all the rest of it? Or does he see his own putative ancestors, the fierce old Israelite warriors of what we call the Old Testament, Joshua and Gideon and Saul who hath slain his thousands and David his ten thousands?

An Awkward People

It has been a difficult time for English republicans. In many a laboured article in the *Guardian* and *Independent*, backed by a readers' army of mean-minded begrudgers, they predicted that the Queen Mother's funeral would prove that people cared little or nothing for the monarchy.

So they had a nasty surprise when the people turned out in thousands to file past the royal catafalque, and an even nastier surprise when they came in their hundreds of thousands to watch the funeral procession going by.

Still, they did their best. What with fine April weather and the notorious English passion for queueing, they argued it had just meant a good opportunity for a day out and a chance to say, "I was there", on a historic occasion.

In any case, they said, the Tory press was exploiting the situation, pretending that the people's apparent enthusiasm for this ceremony showed a genuine devotion to the monarchy. Which, of course, proved that even a genuine devotion to the monarchy must mean nothing.

A glum editorial in the *Independent* made the best of things: "There is no great popular demand for an elected president, but there is a continuing sense that the remnants of the old 'magical' monarchy are out of step with democratic values. The process of modernisation must proceed apace."

This is the precise opposite of the truth. What person in his senses would willingly exchange the benign and wholesome magic of the monarchy for the leaden democratic values of a Blairite socialist dictatorship? The message and heartfelt cry that came from the London crowd was a message that the crowd itself perhaps only half understood: "O Lord, save us from unremitting change. But if all else must change, at least spare for our comfort this one thing."

Tradition

Back in the real world, it seems there is a custom in the Metropolitan Police by which officers late on duty have to buy doughnuts for their colleagues. For being only a few minutes late they may have to buy as many as 400 doughnuts, costing as much as £200.

A few disgruntled recruits are complaining of the expense and even going sick to avoid it, so this beautiful old custom may be abolished.

Must all tradition perish before the onrush of ravening, cost effective modernity?

Fortunately, there are some police forces where ritual and custom are paramount. Nerdley Police, for example, have an ancient custom by which officers late on duty have to pay a fine of up to 500 chocolate éclairs and eat them at a sitting.

According to another old custom, the Stretchford police fan club supremo, Det Supt J.S. Harrogate, must always keep a plate of cold meat and an apricot tart on his desk. At the end of a fortnight, the food is distributed to the poor and homeless and replaced. Officers who fail to salute the tart pay a forfeit in sardines or anchovies.

This is only one of many old customs you can read about in R.S. Sheep-Harris's *Highways and Byways in the Greater Stretchford Police Area* (Sadcake Press, £14.99), "a moving treasure-house", as the author notes in his preface, "of much that has come down to us from the mist-enshrouded haunts of immemorial antiquity".

People and Parties

Isn't it wonderful news (writes Jill le Briggs) that Zahir Shah, the former King of Afghanistan, has returned from exile in Rome to sort things out? By all accounts, he is a real sweetie-pie, star of the Rome party scene at 87, and can charm the birds off the trees. If he can't sort things out, nobody can.

Isn't it wonderful, too, that in June he's going to summon a loya jirga, the traditional tribal gathering of all the Afghan elders! The last loya jirga was held donkeys' years ago, but everyone who was there tells me it was a feast of fun and fashion, ablaze with handsome men in gorgeous uniforms and glamorous women, top heavy with jewels, in gaily coloured burqas, and a fabulous display of guns and other weapons. The only thing is: why does the LJ have to be held in some dustbowl like Kabul or Kandahar or, worse still, at some one-horse dump like Khost, Gardez, Gomez or whatever? Last year's gathering of Afghan bigshots wasn't held in Afghanistan at all, but in Germany.

So why not be enterprising for once and hold it in Harrogate, a lovely Yorkshire town that's awash with conference facilities and all kinds of first-class tourist attractions? Why not have a pop festival at the same time, with glam parties stuffed with TV celebs, star footballers, models and all the beautiful people?

This would help to bring Afghanistan out of the Dark Ages and into the real world at last, with terrific consequences for world peace and prosperity and other worthy causes. Personally, I can't wait for June. See you at Betty's Tearooms!

Shock Horror Bid

When I heard about M. Le Pen's success in the French presidential election, a slight rictus, almost the beginning of a smile, might have been seen spreading over part of my normally impassive features, while a deep sepulchral noise resembling a laugh might have been heard. This reaction seems not to have been shared by many.

"The monster lives!" wrote one eminent journalist. "With stiff limbs plundered from the charnel house of European history ... bile transfused from warriors who fell in foolish causes ... the creature is loosed upon the earth ... Jean-Marie Le Pen is fascism's Frankenstein." And that was not the half of it.

From other authorities came equally unfavourable, though less excitingly gothic assessments. "It throws a dirty great rock into the European political pool" (Neil Kinnock); "repellent policies" (Tony Blair); "ghastly and extreme motivations" (Iain Duncan Smith); a universal condemnation of "Right-wing extremism" wherever it might be found.

Much of my pleasure in Le Pen's success came from the dismay and alarm of all those orthodox Left-liberal politicians and thinkers. Millions of Frenchmen have voted for a man who actually dared to point out the overriding importance of mass immigration for France and Europe, and the connection of that immigration with growing crime and disorder. How dare they? Where will this "Right-wing extremism" end?

What about "Right-wing extremists" ("backwoodsmen", "fascists", "neo-Nazis" etc) here in England? They are mostly the quite respectable people who not long ago were known as "Conservatives", plus other quite respectable people who, as they say, "have always voted Labour because our forebears voted Labour", but are now beginning to have doubts. Altogether there are a lot of them. They may even be the majority.

We peer across the Channel (or through the Channel Tunnel), thinking dangerous thoughts and wondering whether Le Pen can tell us anything. An English Le Pen, being English, would of course be quite different and greatly superior to that rather unpleasing Frenchman. He might be leader of a party which could once again be called Conservative.

Is This Your Name?

If your name is Stomach, you will be relieved to know that it has no connection with the digestive system. It is derived from Stummock, a coarse, spiked grass found in Galloway, Scotland, and was applied to people who gathered it either for food or for therapeutic basket-making.

Tinnitus is one of a group of misleadingly medical-sounding surnames. It is of Cornish origin and means "one who is forever examining the contents of a Cornish pasty in a tiresomely critical manner", an indication of the idiomatic richness and complexity of the old Cornish language.

If your name is Hernia, there is no need for embarrassment. Mocking or ironically sympathetic friends are merely showing their ignorance. The name is derived from Heroner, a man whose job it was to watch herons near the fishponds on a medieval estate and deter them from taking all the fish.

Membrane, a surname common in parts of Worcestershire, is derived from Numbrain, a name applied to people thought to have slow reactions.

If your name is Sphygmomanometer, you should consult a physician.

With the Nodules

Harry and Janet Nodule, the well-known traffic-jam fans of Turgis Hill in South London, stared out of the window at their Boggs Snail Saloon standing forlornly in the rainy street. Should they take it out today in the hope of finding a good snarl-up? The lower part of the front of Janet's head had a sort of tense look, and the two small apertures in the upper part were all screwed up and almost invisible.

In a droning voice, Harry was reading aloud from an old newspaper, as he often does, tracing the words with one of the chipolata sausage-shaped projections on his right hand. Suddenly he stopped dead. "Do you know, Janet, it says here that they're going to use satellites to track us motorists on some roads and charge us for periods of what they call 'congestion'. Would you believe it?"

The apertures in the upper part of Janet's face opened up in a sort of surprise. "You mean we're going to have to pay for our traffic-jams? Oh dear, how can we ever afford it? We'll have to give it all up, and then, oh

Harry, what shall we do with our lives?"

"Don't worry, dear, we'll manage somehow," Harry said reassuringly, though he was equally aghast at the thought of the empty future before them. "We'll save up by going without food every other week. We'll get part-time work in a road-rage remedial centre.

"But," he said as a thought struck him, "I've read in *Gridlock*, the weekly magazine for all traffic jam fans, that 12,000 top British and American scientists believe traffic-jams are valuable for promoting meditation, spiritual development and all-round health." A strange, pallid light began to play about the front of his head, which was quivering all over.

"Perhaps we'll get doctor to prescribe a good snarl-up once a week, free on the NHS," he murmured, scratching the top of his head where it comes to a marked point.

Higher Education

The crisis in university education has not spared the "Big Three" of the Stretchford Conurbation — Stretchford, Nerdley and Soup Hales — or the dozens of others — former polytechnics ranging from Carbon Brush Road University to the Democratic University of Lampton-Upon-Hoke.

Everywhere academic staff have been cut, though the more essential jobs — porters, storekeepers, waste disposal co-ordinators — have suffered less. In Nerdley University alone, the engineering department has lost 145 jobs. Its laboratory equipment is reduced to a couple of condom-vending machines.

The physics department has lost 134 jobs and its equipment now consists of a single ice lolly-making machine. The department of molecular biology has been wiped out altogether. All that remains is a sinister looking uncontrollable livid green growth of genetically modified poison ivy.

Arts faculties have been decimated, though such disciplines as road rage studies, alcopop studies, fat cat studies, media studies and underwater motorcycling heritage studies, for which there is an irresistible demand, are comparatively untouched.

In Stretchford itself, the huge complex of universities in the Canal Road area, St Oick's being pre-eminent with a whole semi-detached house to itself, has slowed down the rot to some extent by offering plain MA degrees in General Studies with no compulsion to study anything at all.

But Sir William Goth-Jones, vice-chancellor of Stretchford, remains optimistic. "We shall continue to meet the challenge of higher education for all, as well as the more focused challenge that encapsulates the challenging ideal of excellence."

What the Papers Say

In a thoughtful leader, *The Feudal Times and Reactionary Herald* discusses the meaning of the jubilee: "It is both gratifying and encouraging that the populace took to the streets of London in such numbers, to express, in their own rough and ready fashion, their loyalty to the Queen and their gratitude for her reign.

"The alien, barbarous and grotesque music performed, against all reason and precedent, in the precincts of the Palace, must have astonished and angered many. But in contrast, the overwhelming volume and obvious sincerity with which the crowd rendered patriotic songs, when the Royal Family appeared in public at the close of the proceedings, indicate that in spite of all corrupting, cosmopolitan influences the heart of the nation remains sound.

"The foaming levellers, decayed polytechnic lecturers, scientific blackguards, doctrinaire socialists and dull-eyed calculators who are always with us are, needless to say, urging further 'reform' of the monarchy on the ground that this is what the people want. As the people have just shown, this is precisely what they do not want. In the midst of change they want continuity, in the midst of turbulence, calm.

"Rather than desiring further dilution of the monarchy, the most part of the honest men and women of this country, we dare aver, fervently desire its consolidation, and with it the consolidation of the hereditary principle, now threatened as never before. Building on that, we may hope in the end to recover what has been lost: the original Royal Prerogative and the Divine Right of Kings."

Art History

Hamish Dreadberg, brother of Neville Dreadberg, the brilliant television director, novelist, dramatist, composer, choreographer and multimedia self-publicist, is making art history as the first director of Stretch Brit, the Stretchford art gallery devoted to British art.

His watchwords are "accessibility" and "relevance". He makes no secret of his contempt for most of the works exhibited, many of which are Victorian and representational. A big notice in garish, continually changing strip lights at the entrance announces: "Here is a collection of old-fashioned British crap. Come on in all the same. You can learn from it."

All the works and sculptures are labelled with appropriate historical notes. The landscapes are interpreted by reference to oppressive landowners who ruled before the days of the people's "right to roam": portraits of royal personages are accompanied by warnings against elitism, historical pictures by notes on colonialism, the slave trade and exploitation of the Third World.

Scenes of rural life illustrate the subjugation of women and the evils of homophobia, animal pictures the absence of animal rights. There is ingenious use of "audio aids". Raucous laughter, eructatory and other dismissive noises and the sound of flushing water closets pervade a gallery of aristocratic portraits.

To complete the lesson, a moving staircase at the exit propels visitors at high speed towards the neighbouring Stretch Mod Gallery, whose director is Howard Dreadberg, another member of this gifted family. Here are works by the greatest creative talents of today: Homi Bhung, Antony Jumbly, Hans-Deiter Zwergendorf, Samantha Dreadberg and the brilliant young dung painter Tracy Goth-Jones, niece of Sir Quentin Goth-Jones, chairman of Stretchford Arts. In Dreadberg's own words: "This is a vibrant, in-yer-face assertion of youth, fun and human rights."

Help! Help!

This week six children, aged from 10 to 16, gave evidence to a committee of MPs in favour of a human rights commission for children, complete, no doubt, with commissioner and an ever-growing army of deputy commissioners, deputy assistant commissioners, case workers, outreach liaison officers and so on and so forth.

The committee, evidently recognising small simulacra of themselves, praised the children's performance. They certainly showed they had absorbed the attitudes and opinions already fed to them by the grown-up operatives of the booming human rights industry.

One child parroted that David Blunkett's remark about schools being "swamped" by asylum seekers was "an example of how the Government did not really respect children and young people". As they repeat the current clichés, these children probably believe they are boldly "thinking for themselves". They have been told that "human rights" will improve their lot, when in fact they are a useful instrument of the coming total socialist state.

What will become of these poor, deluded children, with their arid, self-righteous, priggish ways? Will they turn into workers in policy groups, think tanks, even the most boring kind of Labour MPs?

The sun goes out, and a mass of chewed cardboard fills the universe. I could not go on, but for the hope that some stern Paisley figure might appear, admonishing them in a voice of thunder: "We have no rights; we have only duties."

People and Parties

What a week it's been (writes Jill le Briggs)! First to Rome, for a most enjoyable United Nations World Food Summit. This is a marvellous conference about feeding all the starving people in the world. It also brings together colourful leaders of the Third World to discuss their own diet problems in a most practical way.

Monday: drinkies with Bob Mugabe in his sumptuous hotel suite. Unlike some of the delegates, Bob was not wearing colourful robes, but a beautifully cut pin-stripe number. What a charmer he is! I was riveted as he explained how, in spite of hurtful misunderstandings, he's doing his best to rid his country of the last vestiges of the white colonial rulers, and using the land they misused to feed his people. Incidentally, Bob is a superb mimic. His imitations of ghastly white farmers and their even more ghastly wives had me in fits.

Wednesday: over to Kabul for the Loya Jirga. The last one was held 30 years ago, and by all accounts it was a party to end all parties, awash with handsome tribal leaders in gorgeous uniforms and glamorous women awash with jewels and gaily coloured Paris-designed burqas.

This Loya Jirga, I must admit, seemed a bit low key in comparison. But the lack of glamour was made up for by a kind of exciting, electric atmosphere. King Zahir Shah, who returned from exile in Rome to be here, is, of course, an absolute old sweetie pie and at 87 was the star of the party circuit in Rome. Unlike Bob Mugabe, he's not much of a mimic. But he can still charm the birds off the trees, and if anyone can knock the Afghans' heads together and make them see sense, he's the man.

I met so many warlords, all awash with charm, that I can't decide which of them I fancied most. Gen Dostum, Ismail Khan (the Lion of Herat, as they call him), Gul Agha and dozens more were all fun to talk to, though I was sorry that Gen Hekmatyar, by report a real barrel of laughs, was unable to attend.

As I chatted with the warlords about the future of Afghanistan, their plans for the holidays, how to make a radioactive bomb and this and that, the fun was somehow enhanced, every now and then, by distant explosions and bursts of gunfire.

Prisoners

Nelson Mandela, visiting the Libyan convicted of the Lockerbie bombing, now in solitary confinement in a Scottish prison, complained that he was a victim of "psychological persecution"; he should be allowed to serve the rest of his life sentence in a Muslim country.

The wily old Chinaman's tenderness for Libyans must be due to gratitude for the support Gaddafi gave the African National Congress when Mandela himself was a prisoner in South Africa.

Unlike the imprisoned Libyan, Mandela was not in solitary confinement throughout his 27-year sentence. He had access to books and was even allowed to give dinner parties where, it was said, prison warders had the privilege of waiting on the guests and were awed by the elevated conversation about Spinoza, Nietzsche, Gramsci, Mrs Dutt-Pauker etc. And all the while, in the pages of the *Guardian* and in the wobbling minds of Hampstead thinkers, he was being maltreated, even tortured, by the evil Boers.

Changed Utterly

"Ireland Kicks Ass!" I found this brutish American locution glaring at me from the cover of the *New Statesman*, of all places, with a picture of a burly, leather-clad, stubble-chinned, earring-ed, Polaroid-bespectacled ruffian of supposedly Irish appearance aiming a hefty kick at the world.

Hastily, I put myself in a posture of defence. Inside was an article glorifying the "new-found affluence and entrepreneurial spirit" of a country that has "transformed itself from impoverished victim to land of wealth and modernity — the Celtic tiger". Moreover, it declared, for all their ruthless pursuit of wealth and success, the Irish are tremendously popular throughout the world; even in England one in four people claims to have Irish roots (baselessly; the real figure is said to be one in 10).

Yes, Ireland has entered the modern world. The Church has lost much of its formerly awesome authority. Its once quiet towns and empty roads are roaring with traffic; hideous bungalows deface its once supremely beautiful Western seaboard. It has lost its ancient language, the essential sign of its nationhood, as a medium of daily speech.

Crime and drug addiction are growing. Dublin, full of smart shops and glittering trash, is expanding to monstrous size. All over this formerly slow-paced, inward-looking country, with its neighbourly gifts of lively talk and malicious gossip, the people sit obsessively watching television, and mostly English television at that. A terrible ugliness is born.

Received opinion in England is that all this modernity, which is making Ireland, once a model of blessed backwardness, more like England every day, is not only irresistible but entirely admirable. Do most Irish people feel the same, or do some of them at least share my horror and revulsion? Are they happy to lose their identity in the new world of money-ridden barbarism?

Was it for this kind of freedom that all those brave men and women through the centuries gave their lives — that Ireland should become indistinguishable from England, and the worst of England too?

Nature Diary

By *Redshank*

St John's Day, Midsummer Day, has come and gone, bringing to the nature diarists' community, as the country folk call us, melancholy thoughts of the inexpugnable passage of time and of the already declining year. In our neighbourhood, St John's Eve is a time when age-old customs, elsewhere, alas, confined to the mists of antiquity, still flourish even in these prosaic days.

Young men and maidens, not to speak of some in neither category, forsake their clubbing to dance in the woodland glades, undeterred by ghostly commercial travellers, doomed to play solo whist among the trees for all eternity, who scarcely interrupt their play to hurl traditional insults from another world.

It is different with the watercolourists who, following another ancient custom, come trooping out from the neighbouring town to set up their easels in the woods, industriously sketching everything they see, including the indignant dancers. Many of them are retired schoolteachers recommended "remedial art therapy" by their psychiatrists, distressed gentlefolk and ordinary people lately released into the community.

All take their orders from the big, ginger-haired old fellow who seems to be their leader. From my library window I watched through powerful field glasses as he rallied them amidst the dancers, lashing out with outsize paintbrush or sharp-edged paintbox and generally giving as good as they got.

He encouraged them, too, with anecdotes of eminent painters he seems to have known well: how he and Turner saw off a gang of criminal art dealers in Petworth Park; how he and Edward Lear, attacked by bandits while painting in Albania, put them to flight by endlessly repeating Lear's limericks.

The village folk regard him with superstitious awe. He lives, so the talk goes in the Blacksmith's Arms, in a rambling old mansion "way out t' other side o' Simpleham Great Park". He is said to be a "gurt old 'un for t' book learnin'." Some say he is writing a "Book of All Known Knowledge". Some say he is the king of all nature diarists. All believe he is a powerful enchanter.

When I called at the inn the other day, there was an animated discussion about him, carried on, of course, in the genuine old British Composite Pandialect. Jack, the retired poacher, told how, when laying a trail of sultanas to trap pheasants, he had seen the big man sitting in his enchanted garden, where creatures of the wild, deemed to be extinct in other parts of England, came to his call: the speckled linnet, the ringed dotterel, the corncrake and the wolf. Jack swore he had once seen an Andean condor perching on the enchanter's shoulder and whispering secrets in his ear.

Old Frank the waspkeeper, who has a tendency to live in the past, and contributes a "Wasp at War" feature to the local newspaper, thinks the master watercolourist is a German or even Japanese spy, using watercolours to signal to enemy airmen. All believe he and his watercolourists are creatures of ill omen, and that to speak to them brings misfortune.

Though I am inclined to smile, I am sure there is a profound rural wisdom here, far beyond the grasp of your average know-all urban intellectual.

Tips and Hints

As part of the Government's campaign to reduce teenage pregnancies, a charity called Parentline has given parents a number of "tips and hints on safe sex". One of them, of course, is to pin up a list of local "family planning" centres about the house or give it to their children.

Another is to warn their children of sex when under the influence of drugs or alcohol. They should leave condoms about the house where their children can easily find them. They should discuss sex and contraception with their children more often.

Dr Llewelyn Goth-Jones, the director of community medicine for Stretchford, has been incessantly recommending these measures since anyone can remember. But he is not complaining that these earnest contraceptive workers have forgotten to give him the credit. After all, they are all working together for the great cause.

In his condom-draped office, while gulping contraceptive pills in a persuasive way, he gives parents further good advice. "Get your kids to watch while you are having safe recreational sex," he says, "and talk it over with them afterwards. Don't be put off if they seem surprised or laugh.

"They will soon learn to talk about sex with you all the time and help to build a condom-conscious home, a unit of the future condom-conscious society, in which everybody will be able to have sex with everybody else, at any time, regardless of gender, age, sexual orientation or criminal convictions."

As well as being director of community medicine, Dr Goth-Jones runs a chain of sex education cinemas and abortion advice centres in the west Midlands and a dozen "sex fun buses" at holiday resorts in the summer. His sex talk-in programme, *Calling Doctor Llew*, is one of the most popular on the GPI Television Network. He is also a director of Malebolge Pharmaceuticals, an important subsidiary of the mammoth Nadir Consortium.

The Old Days

When "Ken" Livingstone was elected Mayor of London in one of the more fatuous and pointless of all Blairite stunts (there is, I believe, a perfectly good Lord Mayor of London already), a deep-toned bell rang in the recesses of my memory. Yes, that must be the fellow I had come across 30 years before, when he was a young footman at Simpleham.

I am not surprised that he should now have been involved in some sort of unseemly brawl in dubious company. According to his fellow servants at Simpleham, he was a born troublemaker, with a sly, ingratiating manner that barely concealed his quarrelsome nature and inordinate conceit. But at first he seems to have carried out his duties — mostly

elementary silver-polishing and place-setting at table under the instructions of Venables, the butler — reasonably well.

It was when he began trying to indoctrinate the other footmen with
his own spite and envy in the form of radical ideas of equality and democracy that there was trouble in the servants' hall. Venables told me,
with mingled scorn and indignation, that Livingstone had actually got a
crony of his, a subversive printer, to produce a leaflet arguing that all the
treasures of Simpleham rightly belonged to the servants and, come the
revolution, would be shared out among them, while the family would be
tried, humiliated and most probably hanged.

This was too much for loyal servants to bear. They knew how to deal
with such people. Livingstone might plead for mercy with his horrible
nasal whine. He was lucky to escape a good ducking in the horse pond
on the home farm, or worse still, an ancient traditional punishment —
the fixture of a ball and chain to his leg by Adam Broadshoulder, the
mighty estate blacksmith. But those were already squeamish times, and
he was simply given his dismissal and sent about his business with a
week's wages of 5s 6d and a cheese sandwich.

Talking of Livingstone, I remember another jumped-up Blairite politician who was a servant at Simpleham in the old days. This was John
Prescott, an under-gardener who looked after the boat on the lake, a rather
surly, stupid fellow, but quite good at heart. It seems he was one of many
who couldn't stand Livingstone at any price, so he can't be all bad.

Memory plays strange tricks. Musing on the old days, I have a distinct impression that many other politicians of today also served in various humble but useful capacities at Simpleham. Sometimes, between
sleeping and waking, I suddenly glimpse the shadowy forms of Cook or
Byers waiting at table. Can that be Mrs Mowlam, respectfully scurrying
into the housekeeper's room at my approach?

As the hypnagogic state deepens into sleep, they merge into the background of panelled wall and moulded ceiling and are lost to view. Not
that these shadowy beings belong only to the so-called "Labour" faction.
Now young Heseltine, the under-gardener, wheels his loaded barrow under
the watchful eye of old Mr Mackenzie, our dreaded head gardener. Now
a ponderous form — can it be Heath, the clerk in the estate office? —
looms before my inward eye, blotting out the light in the Great Library.

As I sink further into sleep, it seems that half the public figures of
today must at one time or another have worked at Simpleham. But with
an indoor staff, even in the Seventies, of more than 200, I can hardly be
expected to distinguish one from the other.

On the March

"Africa for the Africans! The land is ours! You are the masters of your continent! You are marching to glory!" So raved bold Muammar Gaddafi, President of Libya, to the delegates at the inaugural meeting of the African Union in Durban.

Earlier he had visited the impoverished people of Malawi, who received him with ecstasy as his henchmen hurled bundles of US dollar notes from the windows of their armoured limousines.

People who know about these matters suspect that Gaddafi may be a thought form projected by Dr Ngrafta, President of Gombola (formerly Gomboland), believed to be the only head of state in the world who, as well as holding a first-class degree from the London School of Economics, is also a practising witchdoctor (Grade I).

If so, the whole story of Gaddafi and his deeds must be the most elaborate thought-form even Dr Ngrafta has ever projected from his laboratory at the Ngrafta Institute of Theoretical and Applied Sorcery at his capital Bungrafta (formerly New Harrogate).

But let Gaddafi beware! What a sorcerer can create he can also destroy. One day, when Gaddafi is fulminating about Africa for the Africans and marching to glory or addressing cheering crowds of starving peasants who have never heard of Africa, the whole multicoloured illusion may suddenly vanish. He may find himself alone in the desert under the African sun, with nothing but his own glorious words to feed on.

Correspondence

Sir — Nobody who understands the problems facing Britain today doubts that more airports and runways are vital if we are not to sink into a medieval darkness in which facilities for foreign travel are practically nil. Yet when the Government announces schemes to expand existing airports and the building of new ones, there are immediate outbursts of luddite fury.

The stop-progress brigade ignores repeated calls for new airports, from people who live near existing ones. Unlike the rural golden age dreamers, these people know they are lucky to be acquainted at first hand with the triumphs of modern technology.

One of the most absurd objections a vociferous minority of reactionaries make to airports is noise, which, they selfishly complain, disturbs them during the day and stops them sleeping at night. More thoughtful residents realise the value of learning to live with noise and enjoy it.

Noise has immense educational value. The world, thank goodness, is going to get a lot noisier in future. People who learn to enjoy present levels of noise will have a better chance of living happily in the even noisier world of the future.

Noise is a human right. We must make sure we all get our fair share of it.

Paul Ohm
Atomdene, Edgbaston

Unisex God

In his wittily entitled book *God Outside the Box*, to be published next month, Dr Richard Harries, the go-ahead Bishop of Oxford, calls for more recognition by Christians of God's "feminine side". He argues that the idea of God as "the all-powerful male boss" has more to do with attempts at social control than with educated interpretations of the Bible.

Back in the real world, the even more go-ahead Bishop of Stretchford, Dr Spacely-Trellis, strongly supports this view. Indeed he was advocating it long before Dr Harries was ever heard of. Perhaps this accounts for a slight note of acerbity in his comments on his fellow bishop's book:

"While all who believe that the Church and its doctrines must become compatible with our secular modern world, will applaud Dr Harries, I would sound a note of caution. When we speak of the "feminine side of God", we must beware of seeing her as some kind of Earth Mother, a kind old maternal figure devoted to the care of children, to ministering to the sick and helpless and to domestic concerns in general (what I myself have aptly called "the Mother Goddess of the tea-things").

"We must outgrow such primitive ideas. When we think of God's 'feminine side' nowadays, we should think of the modern woman's demand for a career on an equal basis with men. No longer confined beneath the stained glass ceiling of sexism, God is present in the daily cut and thrust of business life, in the wonders of the information revolution, and, above all, in the upward endeavours of our splendid women entrepreneurs.

"God is present in the women, glorious in their smart 'power dressing', who sit on the board of mighty business empires, in a position, after millennia of servitude, to show their male colleagues what social control can really mean. There is a lesson here for all who have not realised that in our modern, secular, practical world, the new unisex God is present in a very real sense."

Humming Along

"Ten miles south across Johannesburg, a gathering of 'Greens' took place near Soweto. A group of Danish teachers sat cross-legged, humming gently, while 30 Korean women marched past, wrapped in a white sheet as a mute gesture of support for their country's trees."

This report from the Civil Society Global Forum, a "fringe" appendage of the Earth Summit, held me in a pleasurable trance for several minutes. I shared the sincere dottiness of these people, inwardly humming and marching along with them.

Returning to my senses, I began to wonder why Scandinavian people should be particularly prone to such odd behaviour. Among the most absurd phenomena of the great anti-apartheid frenzy of the 1980s were sympathisers in Stockholm, teachers most likely, performing the toyi-toyi dance favoured by black demonstrators in South Africa. How their pale Swedish arms, like sea-polyps, swayed and wavered insubstantially in the northern air!

How has the fury of the Northmen, which made Britain quail 1,200 years ago, changed into this mild, daft benevolence? Might it suddenly change again, with Danish teachers, instead of humming, bawling the bloodthirsty war songs of their ancestors and terrifying the global capitalists?

As for the 30 Korean women, how did they contrive to march as one, wrapped in a single white sheet — a feat which would baffle the most expert drill sergeant? And did the trees, back home in Korea, take heart and gratefully put out new green shoots?

Birdbath's Bane

It did not take long for Mr Shuttleworth, Julian Birdbath's neighbour, poultry farmer, part-time literary agent and Job's comforter, to let the

unfortunate author know that a new film
adaptation of *Wuthering Heights* presents
Heathcliff as a woman. Not that the man
who discovered the "missing Bronte sister"
Doreen and now lives, forgotten by the
world, in a disused leadmine in Derbyshire,
was altogether surprised.

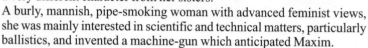

Doreen Bronte, as he discovered, was
a very different character from her sisters.
A burly, mannish, pipe-smoking woman with advanced feminist views,
she was mainly interested in scientific and technical matters, particularly
ballistics, and invented a machine-gun which anticipated Maxim.

For her sisters' literary pursuits she had nothing but amused contempt. Finding them at their books, she would often fling the windows
wide open for "a breath of fresh air", which may have contributed to
their early deaths. As Birdbath found, she produced a lot of miscellaneous scientific papers which her sisters found lying about the parsonage
after she left for America. Only half-understanding them, they reworked
parts of them into the romantic novels we know.

Could the film people, in their confused way, have somehow lighted
on Birdbath's book and connected the figure of Heathcliff, originally a
case study in Doreen's paper *Race, Sex and Class Discrimination in a
West Riding Parish*, into a formidable film heroine?

It was no consolation for Birdbath, who has never received any credit
for his discoveries. As he sat disconsolate at his rusting typewriter, working at his never-to-be completed *Life of Stephen Spender*, with his sole
friend and companion, the toad Amiel, at his side, he fell into a half-
dream. The monstrous female Heathcliff seemed to swell up, menacing
him with her knobbly fists and bawdy laughter, until the crash of a falling
stalactite woke and released him into the dismal reality of the mine.

What the Papers Say

In a thoughtful leader, *The Feudal Times and Reactionary Herald*
discusses the present crisis: "With characteristic impetuosity and vigour,
the North American rebel colonists are now set on the invasion and
conquest of Mesopotamia. As their ambitions widen, they may well follow
it with the occupation of the Levant, Arabia, Persia and the whole
contiguous region.

"The Blairite government seems determined, to the extent of its small ability, to assist the colonists in this bold, far-reaching design. For those who recall the revolt of the colonists more than 200 years ago, what a lamentable reversal of historical roles!

"Things being as they are, we should at least claim some share in their counsels and ensure that they temper their rage for innovation with some prudent regard for the past. Supposing their campaign successful and the entire region subjugated, what are the prospects for its future peace and wellbeing?

"The restoration of the Ottoman Empire (as many will recall, we enjoyed cordial relations with the Sublime Porte as recently as the time of the Crimean War) would surely be welcomed by the most part of the Arab population as promising toleration and good government and an end to confusion and fantasy.

"The restoration of the Caliphate at Baghdad, perhaps with Lord Owen or some other distinguished English statesman as Caliph, would also be popular, we believe, with the proverbial 'man in the dried-up wadi', promising to unite the glory of Haroun al-Rashid with the splendours of ancient Babylon and the enchantments of the *Arabian Nights*.

"In a general settlement the vexed question of a National Home for the Jews must be taken into account, as well as the future status of the Muslim population in Africa, in Pakistan, in the Far East and indeed in Burnley and Huddersfield."

Nature Diary

By *Redshank*

In the mild autumn sunshine the village women sally forth from thatched cottages or disused telephone kiosks for the annual spindleberry gathering. As they search both in likely and unlikely places for the coveted coral pink berries, tempers fray, poke-bonnets are torn, rush-woven baskets go flying and words are spoken which affront and disgust any creatures of the wild that have rashly stayed to listen.

Like most things in our neighbourhood, the origin of spindleberry gathering is lost in the midsts of antiquity. According to tradition, handed down through generations of wise women and herb cultivators, spindleberries, when seethed in an infusion of comfrey, sour milk and Solomon's bedstraw, have a simultaneous binding and loosening effect on the bowels, with no perceptible result whatever.

Is it for this reason that the country folk hold these berries in such high esteem. "Spindleberry juice at night, us'n be all right" is a common saying. I have known a man as mild-tempered as Old Jim, the retired piano tuner, knock an old friend senseless for daring to question the spindleberry's virtues.

Old Dr Higgs, long retired from practice in Bournemouth to live in the Victorian villa called "The Hollies" at the far end of our village, has vainly tried to talk the people out of this obsession, pointing out that there are many other substances that also have no effect whatever and are obtainable without stirring from the average doorstep.

"Tes arl very well for such as 'ee, doctor," Old Jim will argue, "wi' your city ways, to fly in face of nature and threaten biodiversity o' spindleberry ecohabitat as laid down in recent European directives. But take heed lest the menace to Planet Earth don't come creepin' up one day and beat the living daylights out o' ye," — emphasising the point with a gnarled, jabbing forefinger and thumb.

I don't take spindleberry tea myself and I can't help thinking that for once the immemorial wisdom of country folk may not outweigh the cold logic of your average shallow urban intellectual, the boot being on the other foot.

Cosmic Impiety

Civil servants, it is reported, have "invented" at least a million people who, for one reason and another, are missing from the 2001 census. They hope to produce a more accurate picture of the population and its distribution in the country than the mere plain figures of the census can ever do. They have added in, for example, more women aged over 85, more men in their twenties, more pre-school children, more non-English speakers and more people thought "permanently hard to count". They have subtracted people in other categories which they believe have too many.

The new Home Office Department of Invented People must offer some of the most coveted jobs in the Civil Service. What could be more enjoyable than sitting in an office all day creating imaginary people and having the power of life and death over them? An official who considers there are too many people in places like Kensington and Chelsea has only to press a few keys on his computer to wipe out whole streetfuls of the sort of respectable, law-abiding people who are careful to fill in their census forms.

On the other hand, he may find there are not enough happy, easy-going black people in Harrogate. He creates a few thousand and then finds there are too many. He kills them off in road accidents or moves them to another part of the country where there are not enough. But suppose they refuse to go?

That is where his enjoyable work turns into a nightmare. Civil servants may believe in their arrogance that they can create or annihilate as many imaginary people as they like. But they will soon find that their creatures have taken on a life of their own and are not necessarily pleased with the parts assigned to them.

A strange unnatural twilight falls on the Office of Invented People. It fills with clamorous voices, some menacing, some pleading piteously to be released from limbo into life. Thronging faces dissolve and form again like hypnagogic images as the civil servants struggle to assert control. In vain. With horror, they find that, with too much creation of imaginary beings, they have become uncertain of their own reality.

It is their punishment for cosmic impiety: they have usurped the place of the Creator.

Shame!

During a fortnight's retreat in Cornwall, I have been blessedly unaware of the "media" except when particularly disgusting events like Clinton's ovation at the Labour conference or the publication of Mrs Currie's memoirs inescapably impinged.

One event, for some reason little reported in the national press, was the annual conference of Mebyon Kernow, the Cornish nationalist party, at Redruth. As a universal nationalist, I had great hopes of this. The delegates did, of course, vote correctly for Cornish devolution. It was the least they could do. But would they, as I hoped, demand compulsory Cornish in schools and the teaching of all subjects, including science, through the medium of the Cornish language?

Would they demand a reduction, if not an absolute ban, on tourism? Would they demand an all-Cornish television channel, or, better still, a Cornish jamming station which would blot out television transmissions altogether — a tremendous boon, incidentally, to English speakers in the neighbouring counties.

They did none of these things. Instead, among other well-meaning measures, they passed a motion recommending a "co-ordinated and non-violent response to Saddam Hussein through the UN, as a step to achieving peace and stability in the Middle East". They thus tried to enlist about 470,000 Cornish men and women in the ranks of English liberals, without their having the faintest notion of the reason why.

Among these dull political clichés, where is the special secret spirit of Cornwall with its ancient mysteries? What is the use of an independent Cornwall if it turns out to be a very minor, priggish, milk-and-water member of the "international community"? We Luddites, feudal oppressors and clerical reactionaries, who have seen Cornwall as a beacon of reaction to the nations, as the saying is, can only turn our faces to the wall.

Urgent

Members of the rival housewives' fan clubs which make life in the Stretchford conurbation even more unpleasant than it would be without them are keeping a watchful eye on the inventories of the possessions of Diana, Princess of Wales, which were allegedly stolen by her butler.

"From time to time," says Mrs Linda Gumbs, president of the Our Diana Fan Club, "we have sent Diana all kinds of things we thought she would like for herself and her home. Where are they now? If I remember rightly, for instance, there was a lovely three-tone purple, yellow and cerise cardie with genuine plastic buttons in the shape of horses' heads and well-known miniature English cheeses.

"What became of that nest of mahogany-type cakestands, and that old-English-type crumb set? And that tomato-shaped tomato sauce dispenser? And that graduated set of purple teddies with tartan bow-ties? Why aren't they on the list?

"I suppose the so-called anti-Our Diana Fan Club scum, to get even with us, will have sent her all kinds of horrible rubbish like outsize baby blue shellsuits, rubber joke crocodiles and the like. But all of us want to know what's happened to our gifts and no messing about — or else."

Ancient Melodies

When John Prescott, described as a Deputy Prime Minister, called on the Firemen's Union to produce "a constructive response to the Government's request for clarification of the extent to which it would respond to serious fires," the union at once accused the Government of "moral blackmail".

We lovers of tradition and ritual and majestic language had resigned ourselves to the loss of the traditional British strike, scarcely known these last barren 25 years. Is it, against all hope, about to come back again? Listen! Stealing on our ears like distant music come the old trade union verities in the old familiar words! "The door is still open at the eleventh hour... there is still light at the end of the tunnel ... we must take a long, hard look at the grassroots of the dispute... we must get round the table in a spirit of mutual understanding and goodwill."

Shall we see on our screens once again those burly figures in ungainly suits, loaded with briefcases and self-importance, stepping emphatically out of meetings with equally self-important government ministers and officials? Will beer and sandwiches again appear in smoke-filled rooms which have long known only empty air and low-grade Chardonnay?

And will lights again burn all night in union headquarters, until a single union leader emerges at dawn to tell a crowd of waiting pressmen that "due cognisance has been taken of our mutual positions in regard to implementation of a possible solution"?

Look! The spectre of Arthur Scargill rises from the grim battlefield of Orgreave, mouthing the old slogans of class war! There is even a wan gleam in the windows of Cavity House, headquarters of the defunct Amalgamated Union of Hole-borers! Are the ancient custodians of the AHU Rulebook, longer than the Bible, Koran, Zendavesta and the Book of Mormon put together, working on some elaborate emendation of the hallowed text?

Freedom Fighters

Is a new phase of the eternal struggle between the Television Licensing Authority and the television licence evaders about to begin? Is the authority even now massing its forces for a ruthless and perhaps final offensive?

New detector vans, carrying electronic equipment of unheard of complexity, able to detect an unlicensed set, even when it is not working, up to five miles away, will soon be on the streets, striking terror into the hearts of all but the bravest. The bravest are dauntless warriors of Telela, the Television Licence Evaders' Liberation Army, embattled in the mountain caves of south London, whence they emerge to harry the detector vans and their crews, matching atrocity with atrocity.

I am one of the very few (reports special correspondent Brendan Templemead) who have penetrated their secret hide-outs, adorned with the severed heads of BBC engineers, where they plan their raids under the command of ex-accountant Attila Craggs, the man they call "El Gran Deslicenciado". They speak in the preferred tongue of the south London guerrilla, Commercial Spanish.

Blindfolded, I was led through a labyrinth of passages into the presence of this ruthless leader whom few have met face to face. "Deslicenciado?" he asked me fiercely. "Si, deslicenciado," I lied, knowing that any other answer would mean incarceration or death.

"When you return to the outer world," he growled, "the world of pygmies and cowards who writhe under the heel of BBC oppression, tell them this! Let the BBC do its worst! I say pif! paf! to their devil's box of tricks! We shall never surrender! Deslicenciadad o Muerte!"

There can be no doubt that he means every word. The drama now being played out on the streets of Turgis Hill and Brassgrove Park is a fight to a finish.

Correspondence

Sir — I note with regret that Peggy Moran, the actress who made her name in the horror film *The Mummy's Hand* in the Thirties, has passed away at 84. But as a registered fan of Brian Hohenzollern's peerless Piledriver Films, I cannot let her reported sobriquet, "Queen of Scream", go unchallenged.

For my money, I would back Kay Wittelsbach, the lissom, violet-eyed particle physicist in that masterpiece *Environmental Zombies*, for the sheer volume of her screaming against any horror film heroine you could mention.

I well remember, I believe, a gala performance of Piledriver's *Depository of the Ghouls* at the Old Odium cinema in Soup Hales, when Kay, recoiling from a swarm of malignant asteroids (played by that versatile actor, Sean Abdul Hamid) which had emerged from an accursed three piece suite, gave a scream of such unearthly power that the seven-manual Wurlitzer organ was activated.

Carrying the hapless organist with it, it rose steadily to the roof, playing *Selection: Mahleriana* (arr. Rimmer) of its own accord, and was only silenced by the timely arrival, as I believe I recall, of the fire brigade.

I hope I am not wasting your time with an old man's memories.

OLD TIMER, NERDLEY.

Moment of Glory

Ever on the look out for new victims of
oppression, Mrs Dutt-Pauker's daughter
Deirdre has taken up the case of the Chechens.
Only a people deprived of good schools and
hospitals, social services and sports facilities,
she believes, would be driven to taking a whole
theatre full of people hostage and sacrificing
their own lives for the sake of their principles.

Seized with the urge to demonstrate on
their behalf, she searched the banner store at
Marxmount, but could find nothing even re-
motely connected with the Chechen cause.
Would "Hands off Nicaragua" do? Or "Open Second Front Now"? In
desperation, she snatched up an old "We Shall Overcome" banner and
set off for the Russian Embassy.

Bewildered, perhaps by the strangeness and novelty of demonstrating against what had so recently been the virtuous and progressive Soviet Union, she soon found herself, as though from force of habit, outside South Africa House instead, bawling "Release Mandela!" A warm
feeling of progressive satisfaction came over her. It was just like the old
days. But why were people staring at her? Why did a kindly woman take
her by the arm and ask her whether she had been abused in childhood?

She retreated to Marxmount to think things over. To help the cause,
should she employ a Chechen au pair girl to look after Bert Brecht Mao
Che Banana, her bearded little activist son? How would such a girl, if
she could find one, get on with Gjoq, the formidable Albanian au pair
whose fanatical support of the Kosovar Liberation Army had already led
to serious violence behind the green baize door of the nursery wing?

With all these problems weighing on her mind, she blundered into
her mother's study, pouring out a passionate tale of the wrongs of the
Chechens. But, as her mother listened, a sudden, unlooked for, overwhelming sense of glory rose in the depths of her soul, mantling her
withered Marxist cheeks and sparkling in her dim dialectical eyes.

The Chechens! Hadn't Stalin himself, as the German armies made
for the Caucasus in 1942, realised that the miserable Chechens were likely
to support them, and banished the whole lot, men, women and children,
to Central Asia? Good riddance! That was the way to treat those rotten
elements, those uncultural, nationalist vipers. Let them starve. Letting

them go back to their homeland after the war was a typical piece of weak incorrect policy such as Stalin himself would never have condoned.

She felt an almost mystical sense of communion with Stalin, as though she could enter into the very thoughts of her hero as he sat in the Kremlin, smilingly signing death warrants for thousands of enemies of the People. She saw the beloved, pock-marked face close up, could almost touch the beloved moustache. For a sublime moment, she actually looked like Stalin!

"Mummy! Are you feeling all right?" Deirdre cried. "Mummy! Don't look like that!" The spell was broken. The vision faded. Though she would have liked to sign Deirdre's death warrant, the Chatelaine of Marxmount merely said: "Deirdre, how often must I tell you not to meddle with things you know absolutely nothing about?"

Research

A study by Cancer Research purports to show that women who drink a glass of wine a day are six per cent more likely than those who don't to develop breast cancer by the age of 80. To this information the medical research community has reacted in different ways.

Dr Ron Hardware, whose team of researchers at Nerdley University discovered "passive drinking", is indignant that this factor was not taken into account. "In a recent series of experiments," he says, "we have shown that women subjected to vinous breath, for example from businessmen at or after a prolonged lunch, are 15 per cent more likely to develop breast cancer."

The anti-smoking and anti-alcohol campaigning communities are angry with Sir Richard Doll, one of the authors of the study and the man who first showed the link between smoking and lung cancer. Not only did he declare, against all the rules, that moderate drinking might be harmless and even beneficial, but he made no mention whatever of smoking, active or passive, as a cause of cancer.

"Sir Richard has always been our hero," says a spokesman for the anti-smoking industry. "But there are few things worse than a hero turned traitor." Extremists of the Anti-Smoking Liberation Army, who maintain that it is not possible for anyone to die except from smoking, are planning to picket Sir Richard's home, while anti-alcohol activists breathe laboratory-synthesised vinous breath on him.

But all workers in the health warning industry are united on one thing.

"What sticks out a mile," says Dr Hardware, "is the need for further research on a massive scale. We need more research workers, more laboratory equipment, and above all more money. A government-funded emergency crash programme..."

Fury Flares

As so often, "Old Timer's" memories of horror films, which appeared in this column recently, have set off an avalanche of angry readers' letters, many gnawed at the edges and ringed with stains of tea and cocoa. One anonymous letter, from a lady in Soup Hales, encloses a small phial of dark-coloured liquid, labelled "Deadly Nightshade, Bottled on the premises, Drink immediately."

"As an ardent fan of the old Piledriver Films," she writes, "I was present at the legendary showing of *Depository of the Ghouls* at the old Odium Cinema in Soup Hales, and I can assure you that 'Old Timer's' account of the occasion is a mere tussore [*sic*] of lies. It can only come from the addled brain of a senile dementiac of that ilk.

"To kick off with, the organist, Mr Harold Barmitage, a former PT instructor, was not carried to the ceiling by the Wurlitzer organ, as stated. He managed to get a grip on a balcony and to abseil into the auditorium to rounds of applause while it (the organ) was still moving.

"I have a vivid recollection that it was not playing *Selection: Mahleriana* but an even more moving piece, that old favourite, Ketelbey's tone poem *In the Great Intestine* (arr., of course, Rimmer).

"If you are too lazy or stupid to get your facts right, then please get some more competent person to do it for you."

Phenomena

Scientists at University College London claim to have created earthquakes in a laboratory for the first time. These artificial tremors, which occurred in 10 cubic millimetres of highly compressed rock, were so tiny that they could be felt only through special listening devices. "These quakes won't make your tea cups rattle," one scientist joked.

What miserable little earthquakes! When I was a boy at Simpleham it was my delight to visit my grandfather in the west wing, where he had his own laboratory. A natural philosopher, as he called himself (the vulgar term "scientist" was not yet in vogue), he had made remarkable discoveries for which, of course, he neither sought nor won popular acclaim.

By the beginning of the last century he had worked out the principles of electro-magnetic induction. His laboratory was dimly lit by a single bulb of glow-worm wattage. He had invented a telephone by which, if you had good hearing, you could speak to yourself and a camera which, requiring an exposure of at least 24 hours, produced pictures of people and places which seemed not to belong to this world at all.

How I loved to watch that grave, kindly old man, green-bearded and wearing a tweed toga of his own design, as he pottered among his coils and beakers and test tubes and retorts! As a special treat, he would arrange miniature "phenomena", as he called them. "What shall it be to-day? A thunderstorm? A cyclone? A tidal wave?"

Most of all, I enjoyed his miniature earthquakes. They were most thrilling when, as sometimes happened, things got out of control, setting fire to the ancient building or causing parts of it to collapse. How we laughed, old and young united in destructive glee, as the estate fire brigade, drawn by white horses, its brasswork gleaming, came trundling up the long drive from the South Gazebo!

Correspondence

Sir — So a German historian has seen fit to describe Winston Churchill as a "war criminal" for bombing German cities in World War II with reported loss of civilian lives. As far as I am concerned (and this goes for all my friends and relatives), there were no German civilians in World War II — they were all fully occupied in tramping all over Europe in their jackboots etc.

I am only sorry we ever stopped bombing Germany at all. We should have kept it up to this day — the only way, as I see it, of keeping the Hun under control.

A CRAGGS
"Bashteuton"
Numbe Lane Caravan Site
Nerdley

Deirdre's Quest

From Marxmount, her fine white mansion on
the edge of Hampstead Heath, Mrs Dutt-
Pauker has been sending letters almost daily
to the *Guardian* and the *Independent*, arguing
that on ethical and practical grounds alike there
should be no restriction whatever on the entry
of asylum seekers to this country. The more
rapidly the native population is diluted, she
believes, the sooner Britain will take its place
in the modern world and play its proper part
in the international community.

For once, her daughter Deirdre agrees.
Lately she had been trying to find another Albanian au pair girl to help
Gjoq look after her bearded little activist son, Bert Brecht Ho Che Ba-
nana.

In Camden Town among the asylum seekers she found what she was
looking for: Fatima Boxha, a sturdy Albanian peasant girl who made up
for her lack of English with vigorous gesticulation and expressive spitting. When Deirdre invited her to Marxmount, she found to her surprise
that Fatima's brother, Ibrahim, who closely resembled her, came along
too.

When the pair arrived in her domains, Mrs Dutt-Pauker could not
help noticing how impressed they were by cedared lawns and other obvious signs of wealth. She could not help noticing, either, how Ibrahim's
eyes flickered over her costly treasures, some inherited, some garnered
during a lifetime's devotion to the People's struggle for peace and justice.

She also noticed that Ibrahim, perhaps from force of habit, was fin-
gering a large, wicked-looking knife. But there he had made a mistake.
"Put that knife down at once, you silly little man," said the chatelaine of
Marxmount, with all the freezing hauteur and undeniable authority of a
genuine upper-class English Stalinist.

Cringing, Ibrahim obeyed, and the pair of them scuttled away.
"Deirdre, I dare say your friends are still somewhere in the neighbourhood. Ring the police. Give my name and ask for that nice Chief Inspector Cumberland. And, Deirdre…"

"Yes Mummy."

Calling All Bores

Next Tuesday (writes "Narcolept"), Tedium House, headquarters of the British Boring Board of Control, will be the Mecca for all aficionados of the yawn game. Once again its majestic indoor arena will be the venue for the Christmas tournament in which paladins of the comatose art do battle for the Herbert Trance Trophy, named, of course, after our revered president, Sir Herbert Trance.

As well as top class British ennui maestros, there will be wizards of lethargy from the four corners of the earth: Jean-Pierre Cafard of Canada, Grant Coma Jr of the United States, Antonin Bvorak of the Czech Republic, Bengt Snorresen of Sweden, R.S. Nattacharya of India and, last but not least, Shloime ben Chloroform ("Glorious Shloime") wonder bore of Israel.

The set theme this year is "The Future of the Tory Party". How will foreign champions, for whom this will be mostly uncharted territory, deploy their artistry to weave enchanted webs of tedium and reduce the cognoscenti to semi-conscious delight? Truly a battle of the Titans!

Will they use the fashionable "gay rights" gambit which enterprising bores are now deploying to such devastating effect? Long banned by diehard elements in the BBBC top brass, this gambit, particularly when combined with Tory politics, can deliver a knockout dose of ennui from which bores on the losing end may take days to recover.

The climax of next week's proceedings will be the traditional Grand Bal. Masqué, held in the great chandelier-infested ballroom of Tedium House, when devotees of Morpheus will revolve in stately saraband or caper in lively polka until the daylight hours. All proceeds go to Yawnaway, the BBBC's Home for Retired Bores at Redhill, Surrey — a most worthy cause.